27

November 22, 1963
WITNESS
To History

November 22, 1963

WITNESS

To History

HUGH
AYNESWORTH

Brown Books Publishing Group
Dallas, Texas

November 22, 1963: Witness to History

Brown Books Publishing Group
16250 Knoll Trail Drive, Suite 205
Dallas, Texas 75248
(972) 381-0009

A New Era in Publishing™

ISBN 978-1-61254-127-3
LCCN 2013942827

Printed in the United States
10 9 8 7 6 5 4 3 2 1

For more information or to contact the author, please go to www.BrownBooks.com.

CONTENTS

Foreword

Hugh Aynesworth was not on assignment that fourth Friday of November, 1963. He'd seen plenty of action the previous couple of years, covering all the U.S. manned spaceflights, America's underground nuclear tests, various military exercises, and even Cuba, which he visited just days before the '62 missile crisis. Even so, on November 22, 1963, Aynesworth was at the offices of his paper, the *Dallas Morning News* because newsrooms exert a kind of magnetic force on the men and women who labor in them and because it's always a big story when the President of the United States comes to town.

In fact, the assassination of John Fitzgerald Kennedy that day in Dallas was the biggest story of a lifetime. It would inspire hundreds of books, jump-start the age of television news, create an enduring what-if-he'd-lived industry, and spark scores of conspiracy theories.

The last point especially bears on Aynesworth's extraordinary book, first published a decade ago and updated here to mark the fiftieth anniversary of JFK's murder by Lee Harvey Oswald. As a science and aviation reporter, Hugh was not among the staffers initially assigned to cover the Kennedy story. But as luck and his own curiosity would have it, he was on the street with some lawyer friends, only a few feet from the curb in Dealey Plaza when JFK's limousine eased down the street and Oswald started firing from a sixth-floor window of the Texas Book Depository seventy-five feet away. From that moment forward, Aynesworth was on the case, initially landing some of the first interviews with key players in the tragedy, later fleshing out the backstory and filling in details with reporting found nowhere else.

More than once, he got sidetracked in meaningless interviews and tips that simply wasted time. But that's the thing about great investigative reporters: When they say no lead is too insignificant to pursue, they mean it. That's why Hugh's account of those first few days in Dallas and what led to them has held up remarkably well over the years and why he remains a painful thorn in the side of conspiracy buffs everywhere.

November 22, 1963: WITNESS TO HISTORY introduces readers to many of the central figures in the assassination story. They include Oswald himself, a deeply troubled vagabond who had spent time in the Soviet Union and flirted with Communism. In early summer 1964, Aynesworth would break the news of Oswald's diary, kept during his thirty months in Russia, and his attempted suicide. FBI boss J. Edgar Hoover was not amused by what he considered a security breach.

Marina Oswald, the young Russian bride brought to America by her disaffected and angry husband, comes to life here as a bright, attractive woman with a heart at turns as warm as Texas toast and as cold as a Moscow winter. And, of course, there is Jack Ruby, the Dallas nightclub owner with connections to some local citizens of questionable moral and ethical standing, who shot Oswald less than forty-eight hours after he had been arrested for JFK's murder. Oswald would die in Parkland Hospital's trauma room No. 2, across the hall from Kennedy's deathbed two days earlier.

Readers also meet cab drivers, Dallas cops, private lawyers, and government prosecutors, some heroes and some goats too. The political extremes could be defined by an incident a month before Kennedy's assassination. America's United Nations ambassador Adlai E. Stevenson was coming to Dallas to address a UN Day celebration on October 24. When the event was announced, Major General Edwin A. Walker (ret.), a right-wing zealot with a large following, who himself was the target of a botched assassination attempt by Oswald six months earlier, said he had booked the same facility, the Memorial Theater, for a "U.S. Day" on October 23. That event drew twelve hundred hard-right loyalists, many of whom showed up the next day to picket and otherwise harass Stevenson. As he headed for his car, guided by Stanley Marcus, head of Neiman Marcus and one of the UN Day sponsors, Stevenson was spit upon and hit with a protest sign.

As he recounted to Aynesworth, Marcus calmed the rattled Stevenson as best he could, then resolved to act, a decision made even more urgent by JFK's assassination. On New Year's Day, 1964, Marcus bought a half-page in the two Dallas dailies for an open letter to the city. By titling it "What's Right With Dallas," he could praise the city's "friendly and kind-hearted" people, then turn to his real editorial point—the dangerous political absolutism gathering force in Dallas. His plea for tolerance of differing points of view by all Dallas citizens sobered the community, Marcus told Hugh, even though his company got a rash of charge accounts cancellations.

Let me be clear: I am a partisan. By that, I mean I'm partial to strong news reporting that gets at hidden truth. I've known Hugh Aynesworth for the better part of four decades, first as a colleague at *Newsweek*, later over the course of an enduring friendship. He's the real deal, a dedicated reporter and writer who wants to gather the facts and the "why" behind them so completely and compellingly that the story almost writes itself.

Almost.

It's said that journalism represents the first rough draft of history—and it's said often enough to have long ago become something of a cliché. On rare occasions, a journalist demonstrates that his or her work is strong enough to earn that accolade and even become a near-final draft of history. Put Aynesworth in that category.

Mike Ruby

Michael Ruby is a longtime journalist who has worked for *Business Week*, *Newsweek*, *U.S. News & World Report*, and the *Milwaukee Journal Sentinel*. He now writes and edits nonfiction books. He is no relation to the Ruby mentioned in *November 22, 1963: WITNESS TO HISTORY* and the Foreword.

Acknowledgments

On November 22, 1963, I joined an excited throng in downtown Dallas, merely to catch a glimpse of President Kennedy in a motorcade—never dreaming that half a century later I would still be writing about it—inexorably tied to the tragedy and its aftermath. The mood, the senses, and the visceral feel of that November weekend seldom have faded. The never-ending quest to chronicle, investigate, and explain the unusual events that changed our world remains vivid.

This book is about what occurred and how—including eyewitness testimony of major events, scores of personal memories, and an often critical view of the more bizarre conspiracy theories and fanciful replays.

I have many people to thank. To Paula, my wife of twenty-six years, you are as beautiful inside as out. In the face of hundreds of telephone calls and threats, through twists and turns, you have remained my rock. To my children, Allyson, Allysa, and Grant, all born in the turbulent sixties, the happiest days of my life were the days you were born. To these four, I dedicate this book.

In more than sixty-five years as a journalist, I've encountered many outstanding professionals and enjoyed cherished friends, many of whom helped chronicle this book. My thanks go to Michael Ruby, Merrill McLoughlin, Bob Schieffer, Jim Lehrer, Wesley Pruden, Dan and Sandy Korem, Shelley Katz, Mike and Sondra Cochran, Dave Perry, Bob Jackson, Gary Mack, Jim Leavelle, Kent Biffle, Darwin Payne, Gary DeLaune, Vivian Castleberry, Buell Frazier, Cartha "Deke" DeLoach, Clint Hill, Bob Welch, Paul McCaghren, Bob Huffaker, Bert Shipp, Eddie Barker, Bill Mercer, Robert Oswald, Wes Wise, Ruth Paine, Dr. Kenneth Salyer, Jim Ewell, Jerry Hill, Marina Oswald Porter, H. B. McLain, Jim Bowles, Dr. Robert Beavers, Dr. Robert McClelland, David Murph, William F. Alexander, William A. McKenzie, Rick Thompson, Frank Terry, Del McLaren, Sylvia Komatsu, Paul Wahlstrom, Deborah Marine, Tony Pederson, Bill Paxton, John Lumpkin, Bobbie Wygant, Peter Landesman, Nicola Longford and her competent staff at the Sixth Floor Museum at Dealey Plaza, and Milli Brown and her outstanding group of professionals at Brown Books Publishing Group.

And finally to Bob Mong, editor of the *Dallas Morning News*, and his staff, including David Duitch and Tom Huang, for helping me finish a video documentary about those closely involved in the events of 1963, thank you, one and all.

CHAPTER ONE

Casual Observer . . . Then a Frantic Reporter

Friday, November 22, 1963. A damp, gray autumn sky hung over Dallas—weather to match my mood. President John F. Kennedy was coming to town. There'd be a motorcade, and then JFK would address a luncheon at the Dallas Trade Mart.

The president's visit was a big deal, the local news story of the week or even of the year for that matter. My paper, the *Dallas Morning News*, one of the most influential in Texas, was deploying every available hand to cover the event—everyone except me.

So what if my current beat was science and aviation, not government or politics? All my buddies at the paper, mostly general assignment reporters, had been talking about the Kennedy visit for days. Now they'd all be part of the excitement, reporting a story they'd rehash and embroider at the press club bar for decades to come.

"Where you gonna be?" asked photographer Joe Laird, grinning and juggling several cameras.

"Oh, Hugh's off today," columnist Larry Grove answered for me. "He lucked out."

Grove was my closest friend on the paper. We had just returned from our first coffee break in the cafeteria, where I had told him it looked like the copy boys and I were the only staff who were not going to be with the president at Love Field or at the Trade Mart luncheon.

"You may be the lucky one," Grove grinned. "I guess I'll get a good column out of it, but . . ."

Grove and a handful of beat reporters assigned to cover the JFK visit from various angles soon took off for their staging areas. Though the newsroom was already starting to thin out, the incessant ringing of phones and the clear excitement of those with real assignments only made me feel more excluded.

I guess I was somewhat spoiled. I had been covering all the U.S.-manned spaceflight launches, the nation's underground nuclear testing program, and various military stories, and I'd been to Cuba just days before the Cuban Missile Crisis in 1962. I was used to action—but it seemed there'd be none for me there that day, unless perhaps a Soviet satellite crashed into the presidential motorcade.

Tired of answering other people's telephones and running down reporters for editors and vice versa, I drifted back down to the cafeteria, got another cup of coffee, and picked up the day's paper. I had at least three hours before I was scheduled to interview an aerospace scientist at Southern Methodist University in north Dallas.

The *News* that morning carried a Metro section interview by our main courthouse reporter, Carl Freund, with former Vice President Richard Nixon, who was in town under his lawyer's hat for meetings with Pepsi-Cola bottlers, whom Nixon's New York law firm represented. We further informed our readers that Nixon would fly out of Love Field two hours before the man who barely edged him for the presidency in 1960 landed aboard Air Force One, then a Boeing 707.

At a Baker Hotel press conference, Nixon predicted his old rival might drop Vice President Lyndon Johnson from the ticket in his 1964 reelection campaign if the Texan proved to be a political liability—as Nixon said he believed Johnson already was. As for his own prospects of running in 1964, Nixon said, "I cannot conceive of circumstances under which that would happen."

Politics was in the air.

An Associated Press dispatch, quoting the *Houston Chronicle*, adroitly explained the major reason for Kennedy's Texas trip. Three year earlier, Kennedy and Johnson had carried the state over Nixon and Henry Cabot Lodge by a paper-thin 46,000-vote margin, a critical Electoral College triumph for which Lyndon Johnson deserved most of the credit.

Now the *Chronicle* reported a new statewide poll that showed Kennedy trailing Senator Barry Goldwater of Arizona, his likely opponent in the 1964 election, by about one-hundred thousand votes in Texas if the election were held that day. Although the most recent Gallup Poll showed the president pummeling the conservative Goldwater nationwide, 58 to 42 percent, Kennedy clearly needed to shore up his support in what was then an important swing state. A high-visibility, two-day, five-city tour of Texas accompanied by popular Democrats such as Governor John Connally, Senator Ralph Yarborough, and the vice president must have seemed just the thing to boost his standing.

Kennedy also knew that to have any chance at all against Goldwater in Texas, he needed to forge at least some unity among the Lone Star State's fractious Democratic bickermeisters. Liberal Ralph Yarborough, for example, detested centrists such as Connally and Johnson—and with some reason. The governor and the vice president were never seen doing the senator any favors. Just the opposite. On this trip they seemed determined to put Yarborough in his place. Connally was scheduled to host a private reception for JFK at the governor's mansion in Austin that Friday night: Yarborough was absent from the guest list.

The senator's response to that snub: "I want everybody to join hands in harmony for the greatest welcome to the president and Mrs. Kennedy in the history of Texas," followed by, "Governor Connally is so terribly uneducated governmentally, how could you expect anything else?"

On Thursday afternoon in Houston, Yarborough had defied Kennedy by refusing to ride in the same car as LBJ. He chose instead to be seen with Congressman Albert Thomas. In San Antonio that morning, Secret Service Agent Rufus Youngblood was gently nudging the senator toward Johnson's limo when Yarborough saw Congressman Henry Gonzalez, a political blood brother, and bolted toward him. "Can I ride with you, Henry?" he asked.

That evening, employees at Houston's Rice Hotel heard JFK and LBJ arguing over Yarborough in the presidential suite. Kennedy reportedly informed Johnson in strong terms that he felt the senator— who had much better poll numbers in Texas than Kennedy—was being mistreated, and the president was unhappy about that.

Years later, Yarborough told me that Maury Maverick Jr., a liberal state Democratic committeeman, had complained to him of being shut out of an airport greeting line for the Kennedys. Maverick also warned Yarborough that the Johnson-Connally forces were out to embarrass him however possible.

"I already knew and could feel that," Yarborough said, "but they weren't going to find it any easy task." He added that JFK took him aside during a testimonial dinner for Congressman Thomas on Thursday to assure him, "I don't think you're going to have any more problems on this trip."

As it happened, Henry Gonzalez was also nursing a peeve. He carped to the president aboard Air Force One on their way from Washington, D.C., to Texas that Kennedy was spending only two hours in the Alamo City while three hours had been allocated to Dallas, then a Democratic wasteland represented by the sulfurously right-wing Bruce Alger, the sole Republican in the Texas Congressional delegation. Alger was infamous for having once voted against free milk for kids.

Gonzalez had a point, but JFK was adamant about showing the Democratic flag in the second-largest city in Texas even though the president seemed unlikely to change many hearts or minds in Dallas County. Nixon had steamrolled him by sixty thousand votes in Dallas. Goldwater promised to show even better in this black-earth redoubt of red-meat and wing-nut conservatism.

A number of well-known national Democrats, including UN Ambassador Adlai Stevenson, Governor Connally, and Arkansas Senator J. William Fulbright, advised the president to postpone or skip the Texas trip. They believed groups of virulently anti-Kennedy Texans, some generously financed, planned to take advantage of the press coverage to make their sentiments better known to the world. The senior Democrats feared that with all the over-heated anti-Kennedy rhetoric, something really ugly might occur, especially in Dallas, where E. M. "Ted" Dealey, then publisher of the *News*, headed the long and vociferous list of Kennedy detractors.

Ted Dealey was my boss.

The *News*, largest daily paper in Texas with a weekday circulation of 236,000 in 1963, routinely excoriated Kennedy in its editorial columns, part of the paper's shrill, right-wing political slant that appalled and embarrassed many people in the newsroom, including me—and I was as thoroughly apolitical as anyone on the staff.

In the autumn of 1961, Ted Dealey and a handful of other Texas media executives were invited to the White House for a meeting with Kennedy. This was not a gathering of kindred souls. Yet a mood of strained decorum prevailed until Dealey produced prepared notes from which he addressed the president directly.

"You and your administration are weak sisters," said Dealey, who admonished the president that the United States needed "a man on horseback to lead the nation, and many people in Texas and the Southwest think that you are riding Caroline's tricycle."

Dealey's insults made front-page news across the country. Kennedy wasn't the publisher's only target. The *News* had so viciously attacked Fulbright during his 1962 reelection campaign that the chairman of the Senate Foreign Relations Committee declined invitations from friends to even visit the city.

On October 3, aboard Air Force One with JFK on their way to a dam dedication in Arkansas, Fulbright told Kennedy that he was physically afraid to go to Dallas. He said he greatly feared for the president on his upcoming trip. "Dallas is a very dangerous place," Fulbright said. "I wouldn't go there—and don't you go!"

In Dallas, U.S. Attorney Barefoot Sanders and U.S. District Judge Sarah T. Hughes sent word to the president's aides that they, too, thought the trip "inadvisable."

The day before Kennedy arrived, "Wanted For Treason" handbills started popping up around town. *News* reporters Ed Cocke and Harry McCormick brought examples to work on Thursday morning. The fliers depicted the president in full face and profile, as in a mug shot. "This man," they read, "is wanted for treasonous activities against the United States." Among JFK's alleged crimes: "betraying the Constitution (which he swore to uphold)"; giving "support and encouragement to the Communist inspired racial riots"; and telling "fantastic LIES to the American people (including personal ones like his previous marraige [*sic*] and divorce)."

On Thursday afternoon, city editor Johnny King assigned me to track the handbills to their source and to discover, if possible, whether similar venom might be spewing forth the next day during the president's visit. Harry McCormick, a veteran reporter who'd once been kidnapped by Bonnie and Clyde's gang, suggested I look for leads in the paper's coverage of a "National Indignation Convention" (NIC) held in Dallas a few weeks earlier during which NIC delegates bitterly scorned Kennedy for allowing Yugoslavian pilots to train at Perrin Air Force Base in Sherman, about seventy-five miles north of Dallas.

McCormick's idea paid off. I located an NIC organizer who put me in touch with those who'd printed the "Wanted For Treason" handbills. "We're going to show Kennedy what we think of him," one of them said on the telephone. I reminded him that the city council had passed a resolution making it a misdemeanor to curse or shout obscenities during a public event.

"Oh, we're not going to shout at him," the caller assured me. "In fact, we're going to have our mouths covered with tape so there's no possibility of such behavior. We're going to be law abiding. We don't want to harm anyone. We just want Americans to wake up to what's happening in our country." Before he hung up, he said, "Oh, by the way, you'll be able to recognize us easily. We're going to be wearing Uncle Sam suits."

Johnny King decided not to print what I'd learned. "No laws broken apparently," he said. "One might argue that they violated the laws of good taste [with the handbills], but I doubt anyone will care about that. Let's not make them heroes by writing about them."

God, I thought, *it's going to be a zoo here tomorrow.*

As I sat alone in the cafeteria that Friday morning, browsing through the *News,* I came to a full-page, black-bordered advertisement in the front section, paid for by a group calling itself the American Fact-Finding Committee. Its address was a Dallas post office box number. The ad had been paid for, we soon learned, by oilmen, including Nelson "Bunker" Hunt, son of oil billionaire H.L. Hunt, and H.M. "Bum" Bright, who later became the majority owner of the Dallas Cowboys.

"Welcome Mr. Kennedy to Dallas," the Committee announced in headline type. They proceeded to attack the president in a series of twelve questions—a sort of bill of particulars.

Question number three, for example, asked "Why have you approved the sale of wheat and corn to our enemies when you know the Communist soldiers 'travel on their stomachs' just as ours do? Communist soldiers are daily wounding and/or killing American soldiers in South Vietnam."

Question number nine asked, "Why have you ordered your brother Bobby, the Attorney General, to go soft on Communists, fellow travelers, and ultra-leftists in America while permitting him to persecute loyal Americans who criticize you, your administration, and your leadership?"

The American Fact-Finding Committee referred to itself as "an unaffiliated and non-partisan group of citizens who wish truth." The only name attached to this anti-Kennedy screed was Bernard Weissman, identified as the committee's chairman.

A brief digression: Bernard Weissman, a U.S. Army veteran from Mt. Vernon, New York, was an admirer of the ideologically extreme Army Major General Edwin A. Walker, under whom Weissman had served in Germany. Walker, a member of the John Birch Society, was fired in 1961 by Defense Secretary Robert McNamara for trying to indoctrinate troops under his command in his right-wing point of view. Walker, a native Texan, then moved to Dallas where he made a second career speaking out against communists real and imagined as well as boosting other arch-conservative causes.

In September 1961, Walker had appeared in Oxford, Mississippi, to protest the enrollment of African-American James Meredith at Ole Miss. He was charged with seditious conspiracy, insurrection, and rebellion and spent five days in jail for his efforts. The next year General Walker ran as a Democratic candidate for governor of Texas with the support of GOP Senators John Tower and Barry Goldwater and other prominent conservatives. Walker finished last in the race but grabbed a significant 10 percent of the vote. In April 1963, he barely escaped death when a would-be assassin's bullet meant for him just missed as he sat at his desk in his Turtle Creek-area residence, near downtown Dallas. Several months later, it would be discovered the trigger man was Lee Harvey Oswald.

Bernard Weissman quit his job as a carpet salesman in Newark, New Jersey—he'd previously sold encyclopedias and costume jewelry—to come to Dallas in early November 1963. Weissman was lured south by a friend, Larry Schmidt, who had extravagant notions of uniting various extremely right-wing groups—including the Birchers, NIC, and the Young Americans for Freedom, of which

Schmidt was local executive director—into a mega-organization to be called Conservatism USA, or CUSA, which Schmidt hoped to lead.

"Dallas," Schmidt told Weissman, "is where the action is."

Together, Schmidt and Weissman conceived of the anti-Kennedy ad. They designed and wrote the broadside and then solicited donations to pay for publishing it. Weissman, in an appearance before the Warren Commission, said the ad was submitted only to the *News*, which charged $1,462 to run it, and not to its rival, the *Dallas Times Herald*. "They are a very liberal newspaper," he said of the *Times Herald*, "and we felt it would be a waste of time."

Early that Friday morning, thirty miles to the west in Fort Worth, where JFK and the First Lady spent the night in Suite 850 of the Hotel Texas, presidential aide Kenny O'Donnell pointed out the advertisement to the president. The president showed the ad to Mrs. Kennedy, who blanched as she read it.

"How can a newspaper do that?"

"Now we're entering nut country," Kennedy replied, according to O'Donnell.

Mrs. Kennedy later recalled to author William Manchester that her husband had something else on his mind that morning. Speaking of their rainy, late-night arrival and reception in Fort Worth, Jack told her, "You know, last night would have been a hell of a night to assassinate a president. There was the rain and the night and we were all getting jostled. Suppose a man had a pistol in a briefcase." Jackie recalled that the president pointed a finger at the wall of their suite and pretended to fire two shots.

Friday at about noon, the Kennedys motored into downtown Dallas from Love Field in the back seat of a dark blue 1961 Lincoln Continental convertible. Governor Connally and his wife, Nellie, sat in jump seats directly in front of them. Secret Service agent William R. Greer was behind the wheel. Secret Service agent Roy H. Kellerman sat next to Greer. He had been informed early that day by Kenny O'Donnell that if the rain let up in Dallas the clear plastic bubbletop that fit over the presidential limousine in case of inclement weather should be removed.

The second car in the motorcade was filled with Secret Service agents. LBJ and Lady Bird were to ride in the third car, along with the chagrined Senator Yarborough, who had no Henry Gonzalez equivalents with whom to hitch a ride in Dallas.

Meanwhile back at the *News* cafeteria as I perused the offensive anti-Kennedy ad, I looked up to see an even less welcome sight. Dallas strip club owner Jack Ruby was waiting at the cafeteria cash register to pay for his eggs and toast. Ruby never traveled light. This morning he was burdened with an umbrella, scarf, heavy coat, newspapers, and a fistful of glossy photos of his strippers, pictures I suppose he hoped to finagle Tony Zoppi, the *News'* night club columnist, into running.

Somewhere on his person there was probably also a loaded handgun. Chicago-born Jack Ruby, né Rubenstein, almost always carried a gun.

Ruby was a regular and noxious presence at the *News*—loud, pushy, always trying to hustle publicity for his seedy second-floor strip joint, the Carousel Club, a few blocks west of City Hall and police headquarters on Commerce Street in downtown Dallas. The Carousel and another strip joint, Abe's Colony Club, plus a third such bar, the Theater Lounge, located just behind the Carousel Club, were incongruously juxtaposed across Commerce from the posh Adolphus, the 422-room grande dame of Dallas hotels. Just a block away was the thirty-nine-story Magnolia Building, above which revolved an even more famous Dallas icon, Pegasus, the neon flying horse, corporate logo for Mobil Oil. Three blocks east toward City Hall, on the same side of Commerce, stood yet another local symbol of wealth and privilege, the flagship Neiman Marcus department store.

Jack Ruby's sleazy pursuits rarely took him across the street to the Adolphus, Magnolia Building, or Neiman's, and I wished the same were true for the far less exclusive *News* cafeteria. I held my breath, hoping he wouldn't see me, and exhaled only after the unpleasant hustler with the big mouth stopped to talk briefly to two ad salesmen, then settled down, alone, at a table about fifteen feet away.

I noticed that Ruby leered at our young cashier in her too-short skirt while waiting for his meal. Now I watched as he cut a peephole in his paper to keep up his surveillance as he pretended to read.

A television newsman from WFAA across the street left his table and steered over to finish his coffee with me. He was an astronaut buff and always wanted to get the latest scoop from Cape Canaveral. We chatted briefly about the president's visit and wondered aloud how the Democratic factions—Governor Connally and Vice President Johnson versus Senator Yarborough—would make it through another few hours together. Even though I had dealt with the Uncle Sam protesters the day before, it never crossed my mind to imagine there might be trouble—real trouble.

As I left the cafeteria, I decided to walk over to Main Street and watch the motorcade ease by. After all, it wasn't every day a president came to town.

A little before noon, the clouds had vanished and Dallas gleamed in the sun under a bright blue sky. It was almost like spring. The temperature was climbing toward the high sixties. Agent Kellerman had already seen to storing the presidential bad-weather bubbletop aboard an Air Force support transport for return to Washington.

From the *News* building on Young Street, it was a three-block walk to Market and Main, where the Kennedy Memorial Plaza with its Philip Johnson monument to the slain president is now located. In 1963, the site was part of the Dallas courts complex, a bunch of nondescript businesses, mostly offices for lawyers and bail bondsmen.

Kennedy would pass by in just a few minutes.

Clearly, it was becoming a bigger occasion than I had imagined. The sidewalks were jammed three and four deep with Dallasites hoping to get a glimpse of their handsome, forty-six-year-old president and his lovely wife, who was just thirty-four. An estimated one hundred thousand people turned out to watch the motorcade.

I walked west on Main to Houston, the southeast corner of Dealey Plaza, where Kennedy's motorcade would turn right and proceed for a couple hundred yards before turning sharply left down Elm in front of a dreary brick warehouse, the Texas School Book Depository. Until November 22, I was hardly aware the structure existed.

The crowds were as thick around the plaza as they'd been on Main. When I saw a couple of familiar assistant district attorneys standing in front of the county jail near the corner of Houston and Elm, I walked over to join them. A number of people on the street were tracking Kennedy's progress via their portable radios. I could hear the familiar voices of local news announcers describing the motorcade's progress out of Love Field onto Mockingbird Lane at 11:55, then Lemmon Avenue, Turtle Creek Boulevard, and Cedar Springs Road, in its serpentine route south toward downtown Dallas.

A pilot car driven by Deputy Police Chief George L. Lumpkin, full of cops and surrounded by a swarm of motorcycle officers, went out several blocks ahead of the parade to alert police along the way that the president was close behind. Next came the lead car, an unmarked police sedan driven by Police Chief Jesse Curry. Riding with Curry that day was County Sheriff J. E. "Bill" Decker and U.S. Secret Service Agent-in-Charge Forrest Sorrels, as well as Secret Service Agent Winston G. Lawson.

—◦—⚜—◦—

Jacqueline Kennedy had been a sensation earlier that morning as JFK spoke to a packed breakfast at the Hotel Texas. Associated Press reporter Mike Cochran later said Mrs. Kennedy delayed her appearance by prearrangement, stopping momentarily in the hotel kitchen.

"Where's Jackie?" someone yelled good-naturedly to the president.

"Mrs. Kennedy is organizing herself," JFK replied with a laugh.

"It takes her a bit longer but, of course, she looks better than we do when she does it."

When Jackie made her entrance a few moments later, clad in a bright pink suit and pillbox hat, she dazzled the already excited crowd. Even a few wolf whistles could be heard. Her husband, as astute in the ways of politics as any man ever to hold his job, discarded his notes and extemporized.

"Two years ago," he said, "I introduced myself in Paris by saying I was the man who accompanied Mrs. Kennedy to Paris. I am getting somewhat the same sensation as I travel around Texas."

When the laughter ebbed, Kennedy deftly delivered his punch line.

"Nobody wonders what Lyndon and I wear."

The presidential entourage boarded Air Force One at Carswell Air Force Base for the thirteen-minute flight east to Love Field, where it was greeted by isolated boos and hecklers in an otherwise adoring crowd. One demonstrator held up a sign that read, "Help JFK Stamp Out Democracy."

But the general mood at Love Field and everywhere else—especially through downtown and in Dealey Plaza—was celebratory. Nobody shouted insults or threats or threw things. Frankly I was surprised given the irrational hatred that I knew dwelt in many local hearts. Of course, the onlookers had good reason to mind their manners. Seven hundred state and local government personnel, from Texas Rangers to Dallas firefighters, were deployed around the city to maintain the peace. Earlier that week, Chief Curry sternly announced on television that authorities would take "immediate action to block any improper conduct." Curry even encouraged citizens' arrests if necessary.

To a person, the spectators milling around me along Houston Street by the county jail building were enthusiastic, laughing, and calling to one another. I heard some people try to mimic Kennedy's famous Boston accent, saying "Hahvahd" and "Cuber" and laughing. Others waved little American flags.

We knew the motorcade was near when the police began, with minimal success, to shove people back onto the curb. Then George Lumpkin eased the pilot car to the right around the corner from Main onto Houston, and cheers and applause erupted.

"Well, Mr. President," Nellie Connally said, "You can't say Dallas doesn't love you!"

"No, you certainly can't," Kennedy answered with a smile.

I was standing with my lawyer friends, maybe ten feet from the curb. As we watched the big blue Continental glide by—I vividly remember Governor Connally's broad grin—a huge black woman nearby burst into shouts.

"She's got my dress on! She's got my dress on!" Jackie's pink suit and hat weren't exactly the same shade as her outfit, but it was close enough for the lady to realize a moment of glory.

At 12:30, we heard the first loud *pop!* At first I assumed a nearby police motorcycle had backfired.

Instead it was an improbable loner, a confused and chronic malcontent firing his bolt-action Mannlicher-Carcano with its four-power scope down at the president from the sixth-floor window of the book depository but a stone's throw from where I stood.

Roy Kellerman in the front seat of the presidential limousine heard the *pop!* And turned just as two more shots were fired.

Pop! Pop!

Kennedy and Connally collapsed into their wives' laps.

"Step on it! We're hit!" Kellerman shouted at Agent Greer behind the wheel, racing toward the nearest available trauma unit, the emergency room at Parkland Hospital three miles away.

As the Continental gained speed, Agent Clint Hill leaped from the running board of the Secret Service car, and sprinted toward the stricken president. Hill would later say it was a desperate and futile attempt to shield Kennedy from further injury.

Mrs. Kennedy turned, saw the agent reaching for the vehicle, and clambered up onto the trunk. Hill believed she was reaching for a piece of the president's skull. She then returned to her dying husband's side as they sped to the hospital, the secret service agent clinging to the seat behind them.

On the way to Parkland, Nellie Connally cradled the governor's head in her lap, whispering over and over to him, "Be still, it's going to be all right."

Most agree that Lee Harvey Oswald squeezed off three shots from his $21.45 mail-order rifle that day. But whom he hit, and where, and how many other shooters might have been in Dealey Plaza at the same moment have been endlessly debated. Thousands of books and an endless stream of documentaries have purported to show Oswald did not act alone. Assassination researcher Dave Perry, for example, reports that conspiracy buffs have identified sixty or more assassins stationed at various sites around Dealey Plaza, including one intrepid gunman who supposedly took aim at the president from beneath a manhole cover in the street. What is known for sure is that President Kennedy took one slug to his upper back. Another round, the fatal bullet, blew a gaping crater in the back of his head. At impact, a geyser of blood, bone, and brain tissue shot into the air above Kennedy.

Governor Connally was wounded, too, most probably—according to the Warren Commission—by one of the same bullets that hit the president. This is the controversial Single Bullet Theory, first propounded by the late Pennsylvania Senator Arlen Specter, who was a Warren Commission lawyer in 1964.

As Oswald's rapid rifle shots echoed across the plaza, the scene erupted into chaos. Terrified people ran in every direction, looking for cover, screaming, "Oh no! Oh no!" Some, frozen by fear, stood and wept on the sidewalks. Others tried to shield their children.

I initially had no idea who was shooting at whom or why or where, except that it sounded very close. When I turned to look around, I saw the large lady in pink, who was so overjoyed by Jackie's attire just seconds before, doubled over and vomiting against a street lamp.

"The president's been shot!" someone yelled. Sirens blared. "I saw Lyndon get hit too," said another man.

That's when instinct kicked in. I was a reporter, and I knew I had to start interviewing people. I had to record the event. Three or four people pointed toward the upper floors of the book depository. Police officers, sidearms drawn, approached the building. Others followed a cop racing his motorcycle up the grassy area to the west of the book depository.

My God, this is really happening! I reached in my pockets for paper to start taking notes. The best I could do was a couple of utility payments I hadn't yet mailed and a letter from Empire State Bank thanking me for opening an account.

Next I found I had nothing to write with. In the midst of the pandemonium, I spotted a scared little guy, embraced tightly by his dad, not yet crying, but aware things were more tense than he liked. He forced a half smile, and I noted he was gripping a fat jumbo pencil, like the ones kids used in early grade school. It had a little American flag on the eraser end.

"Hey, I'll give you fifty cents for that pencil," I said, perhaps a little too eagerly. His father gave me a look of deep suspicion.

"Sure!" said the boy, grabbing my quarters as I clutched the ridiculous-looking pencil and plunged through the panicked crowd toward the book depository, grabbing witnesses and digging willy-nilly into the mass confusion.

"Get Him, Kill Him," The Crowd Chanted

From a quarter past eight until nine on the morning of November 22, FBI Special Agent James Patrick Hosty Jr., known as Joe, and forty or so other agents gathered in the Dallas office for their regular biweekly meeting with Special Agent in Charge (SAC) J. Gordon Shanklin. He told the group that if they picked up any indication of trouble for Kennedy's trip, they were immediately to notify the Secret Service, and they were to put it in writing.

After the meeting, Hosty and two other agents met on unrelated matters, finishing up at a quarter to twelve, when Hosty headed out, hoping to get a glance at JFK in the motorcade. "I noticed it was coming up Main Street," the eleven-year veteran of the bureau told the Warren Commission a few weeks later. "That was the only thing I was interested in, where maybe I could watch it if I had a chance."

Joe Hosty did see President Kennedy glide by on Main Street, and then the agent stepped across the street for a bite at the Alamo

Grill, a lunch counter. Minutes later, a waitress conveyed the dreadful news to him—the president had been shot.

Hosty was ordered to head at once to Parkland Hospital. He found the presidential limousine pulled up to the Parkland emergency room. Governor Connally, who'd suffered serious and perplexing wounds to his back, rib, chest as well as inside and outside his right wrist had been wheeled by gurney into Trauma Room No. 2 and then into surgery.

Kennedy, his head and shoulder covered by Clint Hill's suit jacket, was taken to Trauma Room No. 1. A bouquet of yellow roses that Jackie had been given at Love Field rested incongruously on the gurney next to him. The First Lady, her pink suit thickly caked with her husband's blood, was at his side. Doctors detected only the faintest signs of life in the president. At 1:00 p.m., Dr. Kemp Clark, the senior physician working on Kennedy, declared him dead. Two Catholic priests administered last rites.

By half past one, a bronze coffin had arrived at Parkland from the Vernon B. O'Neal funeral home, and soon thereafter President Kennedy was en route back to Love Field, accompanied by his wife.

Dallas County Medical Examiner Earl Rose protested that, according to Texas law, the president's body must be autopsied in Texas. Federal agents effectively ignored Dr. Rose, whose role in the case nevertheless was not over. There were more shooting deaths to come.

In the immediate aftermath of the Kennedy assassination, the sidewalk and street in front of the book depository were all mine for about two minutes. It took that long for the motorcade press corps to fan out from their vehicles as Agent Greer gunned the bloody Continental convertible toward Parkland Hospital. Chief Curry and the carload of Secret Service agents trailed behind. Dozens of other reporters immediately abandoned their original assignments around the city to converge on Dealey Plaza.

Spot news is not for the fainthearted, particularly if the event is a presidential assassination. Suddenly every reporter in Dallas was chasing the biggest story of his or her life. The pressure to get the story right that day was heightened by a good deal of competition to get it first. It was the press at its best and worst.

There were the police to contend with as well. Some intrepid reporters, including my *News* colleague Kent Biffle and television reporter Tom Alyea, ran inside the book depository in search of the shooter, only to find themselves trapped when officers sealed off the building. "The police were eager to lock that door behind us," Biffle recalled afterward, "and they did that, and so they were stuck with us. You know, what were they going to do—throw us out a window?"

Biffle ran for a phone, to check back with the City Desk.

"There was a phone in the office with buttons for two lines," he remembers. "I grabbed it and put it to my ear. A man was telling his broker to 'sell everything except Telephone.' I tried the other line. Another man was giving his broker similar instructions."

As he ran out of an office, two cops with riot guns threw down on the scared reporter.

Later, Kent witnessed, and Alyea photographed, the discovery of the Mannlicher-Carcano, which Oswald had stuffed into a pile of boxes and crates.

WFAA executive Pierce Allman came to Dealey Plaza that day as I had, as a spectator. Allman heard three evenly spaced shots and watched dumbfounded as Kennedy was hit. He recalled thinking, "I just saw the president shot in front of me. That just can't be!" Allman ran toward what would become known as the grassy knoll, stopping briefly when he saw Bill and Gayle Newman lying on the hillside, protecting their two- and four-year-old boys with their bodies.

"Are you OK?" he asked.

"We are," they replied, "but they blew the side of the president's face away."

The WFAA radio executive collected himself sufficiently to realize he needed to call his station immediately. He ran to the nearest structure, the book depository, hoping to find an open pay phone in the lobby. As Allman ran into the building, he encountered a sallow-faced young man and asked him where the nearest phone might me. "He shrugged and pointed further inside, and I hurried off to make a call to the station." Two weeks later, Secret Service agents came by to interview Allman. According to them, the sallow stranger he'd met that day undoubtedly was Lee Harvey Oswald on his way out the door.

Outside of the building, the police did their utmost not only to protect the general crime scene but also to insulate potentially valuable witnesses from the press. Of the eight or so people I first tried to interview around the book depository, the most important was Howard Brennan, a steamfitter—he had his hard hat with him—who was stationed directly across the street opposite Lee Harvey Oswald perched in the sixth-floor window. Brennan watched in amazement as the shooter aimed and fired, then calmly aimed and fired again and again.

The first police APB (all points bulletin) came at a quarter to one and was based on Brennan's description of the shooter.

> *Attention all squads.*
> *Attention all squads.*
> *The suspect in the shooting at Elm and Houston is reported to be an unknown white male, approximately thirty, slender build, height five feet ten inches, weight 165 pounds, reported to be armed with what is thought to be a .30-caliber rifle.*

I saw Brennan talking to two officers and tried to poke my nose into their conversation. "I saw him up there in that window," I heard him say as he pointed toward Oswald's sniper nest. "No doubt he was the one. He wasn't even in much of a hurry."

One cop asked if Brennan could describe the shooter. "Of course," he answered. "I saw him real good."

Then Brennan noticed me and moved away, asking the officers as he did so to keep me and the other reporters away from him—a request they were glad to fulfill. Brennan, I later learned, feared talking to the press lest he endanger himself or his family. Who knew what accomplices the assassin might have? In fact, for that reason he hesitated to identify Oswald positively in the later police line-up.

Several witnesses hurriedly shared a few comments with me. Some feared being quoted by name. One woman said she worked in the depository building, "and I'll be damned if I am going to tell you what I believe."

Sometime during the early moments, I saw a man with a rifle in one of the windows of the depository. Before I thought about what I was doing, I ducked to the pavement—tearing my trousers on a piece of lumber with a nail in it. The next moment I felt like a fool when a cop on the street said something to the man in the window, another Dallas cop who casually leaned out the window to reply.

Next, I caught sight of Paul Rosenfield, a talented feature writer for the *Times Herald* and a regular in our weekly poker game. Paul was standing with four or five other *Times Herald* staffers near the front of the book depository in what appeared to be an ad hoc editorial meeting. Hoping to spy a bit on the competition, I cautiously sidled over. But Rosenfield spotted me and cocked a fist, threatening to punch me out. "Get out of here, *Dallas News* guy," he yelled.

And I did.

Just then I hooked up with a friendlier face, Jim Ewell, our daytime police reporter. As we stood there on the sidewalk, a cop Jim knew walked up. "They've probably got him trapped up there," he said, pointing toward the top of the building. "So damned many places to hide in there."

Reliable information was at a premium. We still didn't know for sure who, if anyone, besides Kennedy had been shot or even if JFK was badly hurt. Naturally, rumors sprouted like mushrooms. A story that LBJ had been hit began the moment Rufus Youngblood jumped on the vice president to act as his human shield. False news that a Secret Service agent had been killed persisted for days.

I made a point of hanging close to police motorcycles and their open radios. In such a crisis, I figured that police radios would be among the first news portals. Sure enough, the one we were standing near began to crackle. Then a male voice rose above the static. "We've had a shooting out here," he said. "A police officer has been shot." The witness said the shooting had just occurred near the intersection of Tenth and Patton Streets to the south of us in Oak Cliff.

I felt strongly that this cop shooting had to be connected to the assassination although I would have had trouble explaining why. I conferred with Ewell, and we agreed that he'd stand by for possible developments at the book depository while I headed for Oak Cliff, a middle-class, mixed-race community popular with both blue collar families and professionals for its easy commute to downtown Dallas.

Ordinarily I would have taken off on my own. But my car was parked blocks away across a wild mass of terrified, confused humanity milling around the streets of Dallas. Time was a serious constraint. So I turned to Vic Robertson, a reporter for WFAA-TV, owned by Belo, which also owns the *News*. I asked Vic if he'd heard what I just heard. He hadn't, but he and his cameraman, Ron Reiland, had a vehicle nearby. They were the fastest way to Tenth and Patton, so I told them about the radio report from Oak Cliff.

"It can't be more than three or four miles from here," Vic said excitedly as I filled him in. "C'mon, we've got a car!"

With Reiland at the wheel of the WFAA station wagon, we blasted out of Dealey Plaza, down the Houston Street viaduct and south across the broad, brown Trinity River bottoms toward the scene of Officer J.D. Tippit's murder. We ran every red light: Vic and I yelled, "Stop! Stop!" at cars at each intersection. We nearly crashed a couple of times, came close to hitting a pedestrian or two, and blew right past one police officer who tried to stop us from approaching the crime scene.

Along the way, Vic pulled a few pages from his reporter's notebook for me to use. I'd filled up my utility bills.

The Tippit shooting occurred just before 1:15 p.m., in a scruffy working-class residential neighborhood of aging frame houses, within a mile of Lee Oswald's rooming house. The more I learned about the crime, the clearer it became to me that it was impulsive, unplanned. The killer had reacted more than acted, and he made scant effort to cover his trail. Nine people or more saw the murder occur or watched as the shooter fled the scene. This was not a clever, experienced criminal.

The greatest challenge in reporting spot news is to gather as much accurate information as possible without the luxury of time to assess how reliable this or that witness might be. The Tippit murder was a textbook case of such a challenge. We not only had to get it right, but we also had to get it fast.

In his 1963 Ford police cruiser—DPD car No. 10—Officer Tippit probably heard the APB about Howard Brennan's description of the sixth-floor assassin a half hour earlier, and was alert for possible suspects. The Warren Commission would later conclude that this was the reason Tippit stopped his car when he saw a suspicious subject on the sidewalk.

"I saw this police car slowly cross and sorta ease up alongside the man," witness Helen Markham told me. Markham was a waitress at the Eatwell Restaurant, a popular 24-hour eatery—where Jack Ruby was a regular—in downtown Dallas. Dressed in her coat and scarf, she was walking to the bus stop at Patton and Jefferson at 1:12 p.m., headed for work, when she saw the man walking east on Tenth away from her. Markham watched as Tippit stopped his vehicle and the man casually walked over to Car No. 10, leaned down, and spoke with the officer through the open passenger window.

Markham was shaken, very scared. When Vic Robertson fired a couple of quick questions at her, I thought she'd break into tears. A man appeared with an empty Coca-Cola case and placed it on the pavement as a seat for her. The waitress gratefully accepted the favor, composed herself a bit, and went on. "I thought it was just a friendly conversation, you know," she said. "But then all of a sudden, the man stepped back a couple of steps, and the officer opened his door and got out. I still thought they were friends. Then all of a sudden, I heard three shots, and the officer fell in the street."

"Did the shooter see you?" I asked.

"Oh, for sure, for sure!" Markham cried. "Strangest thing. He didn't run. He didn't seem scared or upset. He just fooled with his gun and stared at me. I put my hands over my eyes when I saw him looking at me. I was afraid he was fixin' to kill me too. And then as I peeled my fingers away to look again, I saw him starting to jog away."

She said she waited until the killer was half a block away before she ran to officer Tippit's aid. She'd been too scared to utter a sound in the killer's presence, but now Markham began to shout as she knelt over the dying cop. "I was screaming for someone to help me," she said. "I kept saying, 'Somebody has killed a policeman! He has killed him! Killed him! Oh God, help us!'"

J. D. Tippit tried to say something to her with his dying breath, Markham told me, but she couldn't understand his last words.

By now, at least a half dozen reporters had gathered around, each firing question after question at the frightened woman. She told the group that the most remarkable thing about Officer Tippit's slayer was his expression, which Markham described as "wild, glassy-eyed." With that, several officers intervened to escort Helen Markham away from the press to a more detailed debriefing for the police.

* * *

It took a little digging to identify the civilian who'd broadcast the initial alert I'd heard over the police radio in Dealey Plaza. Domingo Benavides, an auto mechanic employed at Dootch Motors on East Jefferson, just a block south of the crime scene, was driving his pickup truck when he noticed Officer Tippit standing by his patrol car. A second male stood near Tippit's right front fender, Benavides told me.

Seconds later, Benavides heard three shots and saw the policeman fall. He stopped his truck and watched the assailant run away. Benavides also noted the spot where the shooter unloaded his handgun and tossed some shell casings into the bushes in a vacant lot.

"I thought he went behind that house there," the mechanic told me as we spoke together near the scene, easily identifiable by the pool of fresh blood staining the pavement. "So I waited a little bit. I was scared. He could have come back and started shooting again."

Benavides said he tried to help Tippit but thought the officer was already dead. "He had this big clot of blood coming out of his head," he said, "and his eyes seemed to sink back into his face. I'd never seen anything like that." He told me that he climbed into the patrol car, grabbed Tippit's mike, and tried to broadcast the alarm but failed to hook up to the dispatcher.

Benavides then left the scene, only to realize as he did so that he'd better go back and show the police where the spent shell casings were. He retrieved two of them, placed them in a cigarette pack and handed it to Officer J. M. Poe, saying nothing about witnessing the murder itself. Only after he returned to work and told his boss what he'd seen was Domingo Benavides finally persuaded to tell his full story to the police.

A later review of the police tapes showed that Benavides was correct—his hurried call had not been registered. The real author of the message turned out to be Thomas Bowley, an electric company employee who happened onto the Tippit murder scene on his way to pick up his wife en route to a vacation in San Antonio.

Bowley said he saw Officer Tippit lying on the street while Domingo Benavides struggled unsuccessfully with the patrol vehicle mike. So he stopped to help out. At 1:18 p.m., or approximately three minutes after Tippit was shot, Tom Bowley broke into the police network with his news. This was the message that I had heard. For his trouble, dispatcher Murray Jackson admonished Bowley, "The citizen using the police radio will remain off the radio."

I next spoke with Barbara Jeanette Davis, a pretty young mother I'd noticed on the street talking with several cops, pointing out to them exactly where she had seen the shooter. Davis told me that she and her sister-in-law, Virginia Davis, heard loud shots coming from the street in front of her apartment at 400 East Tenth.

Peering out the living room window to check out the ruckus, both women saw a young man drop some spent shells and quickly walk away. As Barbara Jeannette spoke with me and a knot of other reporters, a Dallas police officer approached. "It'd be better, young lady, if you didn't talk to reporters anymore," he said. "We're going to want you to draw us a sketch of what you saw, and we don't want you getting mixed up."

I could have told the cop he was way late. Mrs. Davis had already spoken to me and at least six other reporters—in detail.

A Dallas County deputy sheriff strode onto the scene, happy to share what he knew of the incident. He described the shooter almost exactly as Helen Markham and the Davis women had and then nodded his head at a taxi driver named William W. Scoggins. "You need to talk to Mr. Scoggins there," said the deputy. "I think he was the closest witness, the man who saw it all."

Not so.

Scoggins hadn't been nearly as close to the actual shooting as Mrs. Markham, but he had seen enough to tell the pursuing police which way their suspect headed. He even briefly took part in the chase.

A few minutes before the shooting, Scoggins parked his cab near the corner of Tenth and Patton. Then he walked a block over to the Gentleman's Club, a domino parlor and lunch spot on Jefferson opposite Dootch Motors, where he watched the television coverage of the assassination as he waited for his take-out meal and a Coke. Then he returned to his cab to eat lunch.

He was still working on the Coke when he saw a lone male approach Officer Tippit's cruiser, about 150 feet away. Scoggins couldn't see the guy's face at first, he told me, because the man was partially hidden behind some shrubs. But Scoggins saw Tippit leave his car and take a step or two. Then, as he recalled, four shots rang out.

"They were very fast," he told me. "*Pow! pow! pow! pow!* You know." Tippit grabbed his stomach and fell "like a ton of bricks," the cab driver said.

Scoggins jumped from his car and looked up to see the shooter walking directly toward him. "I sorta crouched alongside my cab, thinking I might be next," he said. "But he never looked at me. I heard him mumble, 'poor dumb cop' or 'poor damn cop.'"

To the cab driver, a major mystery was the exceptional speed with which an ambulance crew appeared to treat Tippit. They were closing the ambulance door behind him as the first Dallas police officer arrived on the scene. "It didn't seem like two minutes from when I called my dispatcher until they were here," he told me. The explanation was simple: The Dudley M. Hughes Funeral Home ambulance was located only two blocks away on Jefferson, so the response time for driver J. C. Butler and attendant Eddie Kinsley on this occasion was practically immediate.

Used car salesman Ted Callaway confirmed Scoggins' version of events, except for the number of shots fired: Scoggins heard four, Callaway five. The car dealer, Domingo Benavides' boss at Dootch Motors, told me he was standing on the front porch of the dealership when he heard gunfire. Running out the side door onto Patton, Callaway watched as the killer walked past Scoggins and his cab and headed west.

"He was cutting across the street, gun in hand," Callaway told me. "I saw the cabbie, and it looked like he was hiding from the man. I didn't blame him. The shooter had a pistol in his right hand. I said, 'Hey man, what the hell are you doing? What the hell is going on?'"

Callaway recalled the killer slowed his pace, as if confused. "He said something to me. I couldn't understand what it was. Then he said something else, shrugged his shoulders, and picked up speed going west on Jefferson off of Patton."

The car salesman walked over to the crime scene where he, Thomas Bowley, and another onlooker helped load Tippit on his stretcher into the ambulance. Unsure if the police knew about the killing, Callaway got on Tippit's radio too. "Ten-four," said the dispatcher, "we have the information. The citizen using the radio will remain off the radio now."

Ted Callaway, a Marine Corps veteran, then grabbed Tippit's service revolver, turned to Scoggins, and said, "Let's go get the son of a bitch who's responsible for this!"

Domingo Benavides told me that Callaway and Scoggins invited him to join them. Callaway "kept yelling at the cab driver, 'He's running up Jefferson; let's go get him,'" Benavides said. "The cab driver wasn't too convinced, and when he suggested I come with them, I just grinned [as] they went off."

Together, the two men ran to Scoggins' cab. "I didn't think he'd ever get that damn cab turned around," Callaway later told the Warren Commission. "I said, 'C'mon fella, let's move! C'mon, let's go! We can get that SOB.' But he was a nervous wreck. He was driving this little stick shift checkered cab, and he could hardly shift gears. That's where I made my mistake. I should have gotten in the taxi cab on the driver's side because I used to drive a taxi after I got out of the war. But this guy was so nervous he couldn't drive, so we lost him."

A short while later the Callaway and Scoggins posse returned to Tenth and Patton where Ted Callaway gave Tippit's sidearm to Officer Kenneth Croy.

At autopsy that afternoon at Parkland Hospital, J. D. Tippit was found to have suffered four bullet wounds, three to his chest and one to his right temple, which probably killed him instantly.

By now it was about half past one, just an hour since the president was shot. Dr. Kemp Clark pronounced Kennedy dead at 1:00, but JFK's press aide, Malcolm Kilduff, wouldn't relay the devastating news to the rest of the world until 1:33, about the time that soon-to-be-president Lyndon Johnson, Lady Bird, Jackie, and the rest boarded Air Force One to accompany JFK's body back to Washington.

I knew nothing of this at the time. Tenth and Patton just then was a considerable psychic distance from the main story of the day. It was the epicenter of a massive manhunt for a particular kind of criminal, the cop killer, for whom brother officers typically reserve a special vengeance. I don't know how many members of the Dallas Police Department believed, as I did, that if they caught Tippit's slayer, they also would have in custody the president's assassin, but I do remember how angry and determined they were. There was a lot of muttering about what they should do with this son of a bitch when they caught him.

Police cruisers, carloads of reporters, and a steady stream of the curious kept rolling into the vicinity. Another scratchy bulletin from the police radio sent me scrambling again. "He's in the library," Officer Charles T. Walker said over the mike. "What's the location?" asked the dispatcher. "Marsalis and Jefferson, in the library. I'm going around the back. Get someone on the back."

Under less dire circumstances, this episode would have been good for a laugh. As it happened, Walker observed a young white male, more or less matching the latest description of the fugitive, sprinting across the lawn of the Jefferson Branch Library. Walker reasonably assumed that the police should talk to this individual.

The runner turned out to be Adrian D. Hamby, a college student who worked part time at the library, two blocks from the intersection of Tenth and Patton. When Hamby reported for work at about twenty after one that day, a pair of plainclothes policemen stepped up to accost him. "Sir," said one of the cops, "what are you doing in this area?"

Hamby replied that he worked at the library. "Well, listen," said the officer, "someone just shot and killed a police officer in the vicinity, and we think the suspect is loose. Do us a favor, go into the library, get hold of management, and tell them to lock the doors and not let anyone inside until we secure the area."

Adrian Hamby was eager to do as he was told. He took off at a run, which attracted Walker's attention to the library, and within moments the building was surrounded by police. Walker led a police phalanx, firearms drawn, to a basement entrance where Hamby awaited them. "There was about twenty or thirty police officers out there with rifles, pistols—you name it—and they were pointing them at me and told me to come out with my hands up," Hamby later told Dale K. Myers, who interviewed him for his book *With Malice: Lee Harvey Oswald and the Murder of Officer J. D. Tippit*. "I got scared and closed the door."

The officers took Hamby's panicked reaction for guilty knowledge. "They told me that if I didn't come out they would fire," he remembered. "You talk about being scared. I thought I was doomed."

As Hamby and the rest of the group inside filed through the door, their hands above their heads, Walker, a DPD accident investigator, recognized the figure he'd seen running across the lawn, and the police moved forcefully to seize him.

"They immediately grabbed me and pushed me up against the wall—my legs spread apart—and frisked me," he told Myers. "I was so scared. I just came apart, and I started crying and screaming, 'I work here! I work here! I don't understand! I work here!'" An unnamed Secret Service agent finally stepped forward to vouch for Hamby, explaining to the assembled police that he'd already ascertained the subject was telling the truth. A disappointed Officer Calvin B. Owens contacted the dispatcher. "It was the wrong man," Owens explained into his mike.

"Ten-four," came the reply. "Disregard all the information on the suspect arrested. It was the wrong man."

By this time, I was running out of people to interview and had the feeling that some who had drifted into the area were not, as they claimed, really witnesses but just excitement chasers who wanted to be part of the story. My hunch was confirmed when a teenager was being interviewed by a television reporter, and his buddy suddenly snapped, "C'mon Jack, you weren't even here. You were with me. I'm gonna tell your family."

Meanwhile, thanks to a report I heard over a radio in an unmarked police vehicle, I learned that a "possible suspect" was hightailing it into an old furniture storage house on Jefferson. As I arrived, I heard someone say, "He's in there. I know he's in there."

I recognized Assistant District Attorney Bill Alexander as he and five or six policemen headed into the house, so I followed them into the dim and dusty building. Part of the group split off to search the upstairs.

For the first time this busy, busy afternoon, I felt afraid. When the shots rang out in Dealey Plaza, I was unnerved like everybody else, but after a few seconds, in the confusion and chaos, the sense of personal danger passed.

Now as I crept inside that old house, I had a feeling a showdown was near. Frankly I stayed pretty close to the front door as the others poked around the piles of used furniture, yelling things like, "Come out of there you son of a bitch! We got you now!"

Suddenly one of the upstairs searchers came crashing through the rickety ceiling. "Oooh," I shouted, as I looked up to see legs dangling down and dust swirling. A couple cops close to me, guns drawn, hit a firing stance.

Within seconds the man—half in, half out of the ceiling—said "Damn!" and called to another cop as nervous laughter rose from several areas of the room. I recall looking around the dirty old house and thinking: Every damn guy in here has a gun! What am I doing here?

I scrambled out to the street, which turned out to be a smart move. The suspect was nowhere nearby. Within seconds I heard on an FBI car radio that a suspect had just run into the Texas Theater, about six or seven blocks up Jefferson Avenue. I didn't see any newsmen close by, and I hesitated to ask a carload of cops to ride with them, so I took off at a run.

As I hotfooted it west on Jefferson, I noticed my stomach hurt quite a bit and realized I was really hungry. I hadn't eaten breakfast because my wife had been suffering morning sickness with her first pregnancy, and I had only coffee at the *News*.

I plunged on thinking I didn't have a choice. Not right then anyway.

⁘ ⧫ ⁘

Oswald did a fair job of making himself scarce from the time he left the Tippit crime scene, about 1:16 until about 1:36, when Johnny C. Brewer, manager of the Hardy's Shoe Store at 213 West Jefferson, saw a man he later identified as Oswald step into the shoe store's recessed foyer. Brewer was listening to radio reports from Dealey Plaza. "We knew the president had been hit," he later told me, "and there was this rumor a Secret Service man had been killed also. The radio reporters were just going wild."

Outside his shop, police cars whipped up and down the avenue, tires squealing, sirens wailing. When Oswald ducked into the front of the store, "I thought it was funny," Brewer remembered. "He looked scared. His shirt was out of his pants, and his hair messed up. Seemed like a man who had been running. He just stared at me a moment or so."

A squad car pulled an abrupt U-turn on Jefferson and sped east. Brewer watched as Oswald glanced over his shoulder toward the street, then without saying a word headed west, to his right. The Texas Theater was six doors away.

The store manager went back to his work for a half a minute or so and then heard yet another squad car whiz past, headed west this time. Curious, Brewer walked out the front door and glanced right to see Oswald about fifty yards away, still walking west, nearing the Texas Theater.

Ticket clerk Julia Postal stood in front of the theater, drawn from her box office by the commotion. Brewer noticed Postal, and he also noticed that with her back turned to the theater entrance she couldn't have seen the young man with the tousled hair duck inside without paying. The situation looked suspicious, so Brewer approached Postal. "I asked her if that man in the brown shirt had bought a ticket to get in."

"No, by golly," replied Postal, who was listening to the assassination news on a small transistor radio.

Brewer stepped into the lobby where he found Warren "Butch" Burroughs behind the concession stand. "I grabbed Butch Burroughs and asked him which way the man had gone," Brewer told me. "He said he didn't see anyone enter. He was busy behind the counter. He asked me why I wanted to know about this man. I told him the man was just very suspicious, the way he acted and all."

Back on the pavement, Brewer and Postal drew up a plan. She would watch the front door while the two men checked the two other exits. Brewer and Burroughs also looked for their suspect upstairs and down but couldn't find him. They later learned they passed within a few feet of the seated Oswald.

Postal declared that she was going to call the police and asked Brewer and Burroughs to stand by the two exits until officers arrived. "I don't know if this is the man they wanted," she remembered saying to Brewer, "but he's running from them for some reason."

Butch Burroughs meanwhile was getting caught up in the excitement. "I thought about getting him myself," the concessionaire told me, "but Johnny stopped me. Told me I didn't have a gun and I might need one."

Postal told me that when she described Oswald, the officer on the phone said, "Well that fits the description, no doubt about that."

A dispatcher relayed the call to Officer Bill Anglin, Tippit's best friend on the force, who at the moment was working his buddy's murder scene. "Have information that a suspect just went in the Texas Theater on West Jefferson."

"Ten-four," Anglin answered.

The first squad car arrived in front of the theater ninety seconds later, at 1:47. I wasn't far behind. As I raced into the theater, I looked up at the marquee above me: *Cry of Battle. Van Heflin. War Is Hell.*

Julia Postal was at her ticket counter. "Oh my God! I just heard the president is dead!" she exclaimed. This was the first I'd heard of it. She'd later tell me she recognized Tippit as a former part-time security guard at the theater.

Entering the theater foyer, I eased to the first door on my right and watched a few moments as two, possibly three, men walked up the two aisles.

Then I noticed two men jump up to my left and head to the door. I don't recall what I was thinking, but I eased back into the lobby and hurried over to the second door as the two kept on walking out toward the front exit. Almost immediately a large man appeared, a pistol at his side. I had already seen too many guns that afternoon, and I didn't want to linger here, not totally aware of what was coming. I quickly raced back to my original spot and peered into the gloomy theater.

No more than ten or twelve patrons remained.

As I eased back to my original vantage point, just a few feet behind Oswald, I watched as two men methodically moved from the front of the theater up the aisles. To my left I watched as officer Walker, who had led the abortive raid on the Jefferson Branch Library, slowly inched up the aisle.

To the right, directly in front of me, Maurice "Nick" McDonald, an eight-year veteran of the force, moved even slower and had braced two men who were seated several rows in front of Oswald and was patting them down for weapons.

I could hear voices, obviously emanating from the stage area, but they didn't seem to make any sense, and neither Walker nor McDonald seemed to be paying particular attention to them. The theater lights were raised slightly, but the movie continued.

"Did you see him get up and move toward the aisle?" Brewer asked me shortly afterward. I told him that I hadn't and later figured out that must have occurred while I was moving from door to door. "It was while the officer was frisking the two men," Brewer said.

Later I asked McDonald how he had kept his cool, knowing that Brewer had solidly informed him where the suspect was seated.

"I had looked over my shoulder," the officer said, "and he (Oswald) just sat there quiet, looking at me."

When McDonald reached the suspect's row, he turned quickly and ordered, "Get on your feet."

"Well, it's all over now," he heard Oswald reply.

Except that it wasn't. Not quite.

Oswald stood up, raised his hands in an apparent gesture of surrender and then socked McDonald in the face with his left fist. With his right hand, he pulled a .38 Smith & Wesson from his belt.

At that point, the poorly lit scene exploded into a blur. A motorcycle officer named Thomas Hutson jumped Oswald from behind as Nick McDonald recovered with a fist of his own into Oswald's face or head. A plainclothes cop, Sergeant Gerald Hill, grabbed an arm. He and another cop finally got handcuffs on Oswald. McDonald later told me that he got his hand on the pistol's firing mechanism to prevent Oswald from firing, which, he said, obviously saved his life.

Another cop grabbed Oswald's .38 and stuck it in his belt.

Just then a couple seated near the melee jumped up and fled toward the exit, brushing past me as they ran. The woman screamed until they were outside the theater.

I remember Oswald crying out, "I protest this police brutality! I protest this police brutality!" There was quite a tussle. The cops knocked him around a lot, and he had a forehead cut and black eye to show for it.

Five or possibly six cops were involved in subduing Oswald. As they marched him out the theater door, they were met by a crowd of several hundred people gathered outside. I have no idea how they came together so quickly. It was only 1:50 when the police put Oswald in Hill's unmarked squad car for the ride to City Hall.

An ugly mood pervaded the chanting crowd. "Get him! Kill him!"

CHAPTER THREE

Dallas Cops and FBI at Odds

I know of just one reporter to whom the name Lee Harvey Oswald meant anything before November 22, 1963: Kent Biffle. Still inside the book depository at two o'clock when the suspect's name was first made public, Kent experienced a memory jolt. Biffle remembered that in 1959, when he was a reporter for the old *Fort Worth Press*, he'd written several stories about a turncoat ex-Marine from Fort Worth named Lee Harvey Oswald.

He recalled the *Press* had tried to connect Oswald's bizarre mother, Marguerite, to her son in Moscow via telephone from the paper's newsroom, but Lee had hung up on her.

FBI Agent Joe Hosty in the bureau's Dallas office, who had a far fresher recollection of the suspect, was dumbstruck at the news of Oswald's arrest. Hosty was supposed to be keeping an eye on Lee Harvey Oswald. He had known for weeks that Oswald was working in the book depository, along the path of Kennedy's motorcade.

"I had no reason prior to that to believe he was capable or potentially an assassin of the president of the United States," Hosty insisted to the Warren Commission.

Later, I would help find evidence that contradicted Hosty's assertion.

Lee Harvey Oswald was what law enforcement today calls "a person of interest." In 1959, following a brief and bumpy career in the Marine Corps that included a court martial for fighting and an undesirable discharge, he defected to the Soviet Union at age nineteen and unsuccessfully attempted to renounce his U.S. citizenship in the process.

But life in the workers' paradise didn't pan out. In May 1962, Oswald returned to the United States with his twenty-year-old wife, the former Marina Nikolayevna Prusakova, and their three-month-old daughter, June Lee. The family lived for a time in the Dallas-Fort Worth area but moved to New Orleans in the spring of 1963.

The FBI kept an eye on Oswald as it would any returned defector with a Russian-born spouse. The bureau noted in his file, for example, that Oswald was arrested in New Orleans in August 1963 after getting into a scuffle while handing out "Fair Play for Cuba" fliers.

On October 3, the FBI office in New Orleans informed Dallas that the Oswalds had left Louisiana, presumably headed back to Texas. Marina and her daughter were seen driving away with a woman in a station wagon bearing Texas tags. Agent Hosty was told to find them. It was a routine assignment—"no particular note of urgency," as Hosty described it—until New Orleans also reported that in September Oswald had traveled to Mexico City and visited the Soviet embassy there.

"Did this increase your effort to find him?" a Warren Commission lawyer would ask.

"Very much so, yes," Hosty answered. "I became curious then."

Thanks to another tip from the New Orleans office, on October 29, Hosty tracked the Oswalds to suburban Irving, eight miles west of

Dallas, where Marina and her daughters, little June Lee and Rachel, born October 20, were living with a close friend, Mrs. Ruth Paine at 2515 Fifth Street. Mrs. Paine had driven Marina to Dallas from New Orleans.

Hosty visited Ruth Paine on the first of November. She told the FBI man how she'd recently helped Oswald, an unskilled high school dropout, land a $1.25-per-hour, part-time job filling orders at the Texas School Book Depository on a corner of Dealey Plaza in Dallas. Depository superintendent Roy Truly later told me that he filled two similar openings the day he hired Oswald—one at the Dealey Plaza warehouse and one at another facility in Dallas. Oswald just as easily could have been assigned to the second location.

Mrs. Paine also told Hosty that Oswald was staying at a rooming house in Oak Cliff. She said she was aware there had been considerable discord between the Oswalds and that Lee had been physically violent toward Marina. According to Hosty's notes of his conversation with Mrs. Paine, she "didn't want [Oswald] at her home; that she was willing to take in Marina Oswald and her two children but she didn't have room for him and she didn't want him at the house. She was willing to let him visit his wife and family but didn't want him residing there."

Hosty visited the Paine household one more time, on November 5 but did not speak with Marina. Nor did he ever attempt to interview her evidently unstable husband.

After Lee Harvey Oswald, a suspect in both the Kennedy and the Tippit shootings, was arrested in the Texas Theater, Alan Belmont, then the number three man in the FBI, ordered Hosty via a telephone call from Dallas Special Agent in Charge Gordon Shanklin to grab his Oswald files and hustle over to police headquarters at City Hall to help with the questioning of Oswald.

As Jim Ewell and I reported in the *News* five months later under the two-column headline, "FBI Knew Oswald Capable of Act, Reports Indicate," Hosty arrived at City Hall at 2:05 p.m. and rode up in an elevator with Lieutenant Jack Revill, head of the

DPD Criminal Intelligence Squad, and Officer V. J. "Jackie" Bryan. According to Revill's written account of the episode typed up forty-five minutes later and delivered to Chief Curry that afternoon, in the basement Hosty "stated that the Federal Bureau of Investigation was aware of the Subject [Oswald] and that they had information that this Subject was capable of committing the assassination of President Kennedy."

Joe Hosty denied making the statement to Revill and apparently suspected Jim and me of fabricating it. He refused my every interview request until a couple years before his death in 2011. Then Hosty telephoned me to say that FBI Agent Bob Gemberling, who had coordinated the bureau's investigation of the assassination, had assured him that our *News* story in fact was true: We *had* quoted Revill accurately. Revill had also repeated the assertion later, said Gemberling. Hosty could have gotten the same information by simply asking Revill himself. They saw quite a lot of one another on the job. I don't know why he didn't except that Hosty detested the DPD lieutenant.

As Gemberling told me, "I don't think Revill just made up the last paragraph and added it to his report that day. The intensity and conflicts of those hours and the feeling that the bureau should have figured out what Oswald was capable of might have been factors in how he worded that report."

A few months after the assassination, I asked Gordon Shanklin why the bureau didn't at least tell the Dallas police about Oswald and where he worked. I observed that the cops surely would have wanted to babysit such a character.

"We didn't want him to lose his job," Shanklin explained.

"Well, Mr. Kennedy lost his," I shot back.

As far as I know, Gordon Shanklin never deliberately caused me any difficulty. But I was told by some of his agents that I was not his favorite newsperson. Some years later, as I sought to expose a famous Texas law enforcement official as a perjurer and thief, I asked Shanklin and J. Edgar Hoover to verify certain facts to which they had access, thinking the bureau would be pleased to clean up a case involving one of their own. Shanklin referred me to Hoover, who sent me a courteous letter of refusal. The official in question later—through my efforts—was indicted and convicted.

···⋈⧫⋈···

Like any powerful bureaucrat, Hoover was always careful to protect his turf, which to the director included projecting an air of omniscience and never conceding a mistake. Max Holland in his 2004 book, *The Kennedy Assassination Tapes*, examined some of the credibility issues such a mindset can cause when, in fact, you don't know what you're talking about.

In telephone conversations with Lyndon Johnson on November 22 and 23, Hoover assured LBJ that "we" had charged Oswald with murder when at the time there was no explicit Federal law against killing the president, only against assaulting him. All charges filed against Oswald were state charges.

Hoover also falsely bragged to Johnson that the Bureau had recovered a bullet from JFK's gurney and that Oswald had been captured after a downtown Dallas gunfight in which a police officer was killed. Further, he claimed, A. Hidell, Oswald's alias, was in fact a woman.

"Keeping up this false omniscience," Holland wrote, "means that Hoover conveys a lot of bad information, or misinformation, while briefing the president."

···⋈⧫⋈···

Newsgathering in 1963 was primitive work by today's standards. Our physical tools in the field were paper and pen and precious little else. There were no personal computers. No commercial communication satellites. No Internet. No e-mail. No tweeting or other social media. No FedEx. No fax machines. Even photocopying was pretty new.

We had no mobile voice links, certainly no smartphones. All we had were land lines. Reporters in the field used pay telephones or nothing at all. If you had a story to file, you called it in to someone in the newsroom who took down your dictation, you looked for an open Western Union office, or if you were lucky, you had access to a private telex machine and someone who knew how to operate it.

The third-floor newsroom at the *News* was antediluvian. The big room was outfitted with maybe two dozen battered gray metal desks, arranged in rows. These were the reporters' desks equipped with clunky manual typewriters and telephones. Mine was in front. I recall a single communal file cabinet standing at the end of each row. There were no barriers between us and no privacy.

One other thing: There were very few female reporters—none, as far as I can remember, assigned specifically to the Kennedy story though I recall Vivian Castleberry at the *Times Herald* came through with a fine interview with Judge Sarah Hughes after she had sworn in Lyndon Johnson as the thirty-sixth president.

To write a story in those days, a reporter had to laminate two sheets of eight-by-eleven newsprint around a piece of carbon paper, roll this sandwich into an ancient Underwood, and start banging away. There was no delete button, of course. No spell check. No Google or other online database to query from your desk. When your piece was completed, you impaled the original on a big spindle at the city desk and deposited the copy in a tray for the Associated Press guy to pick up.

On a typical day, a reporter hung around until the piece was edited and sent to the copy desk and beyond, which to most reporters was *terra incognita*. Few of us had more than a rudimentary idea of how a newspaper was assembled, printed, and distributed.

November 22, 1963, was not a typical newsroom day, of course. Not only was the place swarming with our reporters coming and going, people taking telephoned notes from the field, and editors barking assignments and working copy, but we were also inundated with our brothers and a couple of sisters from the national media. As many as a hundred of them descended on us like locusts and were soon about as welcome.

Under deadline pressure, those reporters needed desks, type-writers, telephones, and text transmission facilities to get their stories filed. Under the circumstances, the editorial management of the *News* and the *Times Herald* were happy to accommodate our out-of-town colleagues. But the visiting press quickly abused local hospitality. Some tried to usurp our desks when we needed them to get our own work done. Al Altwegg, business editor at the *News*, nearly started a fistfight with a White House correspondent from *The New York Times* who commandeered Al's desk and wouldn't give it up.

Then there was the assault on our reference department. This spacious facility, filled with desks and chairs, offered access to practically any periodical imaginable, plus the invaluable local news clip files, arranged by name and subject in envelopes, which enabled a reporter quickly to find background information on everything from Police Chief Curry's recent pronouncements to the history of Dealey Plaza.

By that evening, the room looked like Genghis Khan and the golden horde had stormed through it. Files were strewn everywhere. Some clip envelopes had been stolen. By Saturday morning, access to the reference department was strictly limited to *News* staffers. Guards were posted to enforce the prohibition.

Over at City Hall, Chief Curry was stirring up a storm of his own. After returning from Love Field, where he was on hand at 2:38 p.m. to watch Judge Hughes swear in Johnson, Curry read Lieutenant Revill's report on his basement conversation with FBI Agent Hosty with considerable interest.

"If we had known a defector or extremist was anywhere in the city, much less on the parade route, we would have been sitting in his lap," Curry was later quoted by the Associated Press.

The chief told me that up on DPD's third-floor office complex, "I was stopped going down the hall, and the press wanted to know all about what evidence we had and why a Russian defector had been ignored along the motorcade route. I told them that there was a rifle and a pistol belonging to Oswald. And I guess I stepped a bit too far at that point. I said, 'The FBI knew all about this man, knew he was capable of killing the president and so forth.'

Within the hour FBI Director J. Edgar Hoover dispatched Gordon Shanklin to Curry's office with a message. The bespectacled Shanklin apologized for being there, Curry told me, but nonetheless insisted that the chief retract his statement.

Curry trusted that Lieutenant Revill's report was accurate, but "at that point," he explained, "I didn't see what all the shouting was about. I knew the truth would come out soon. But when Shanklin told me the bureau had not had Oswald under surveillance, I agreed, and did soften that statement a few minutes later."

Shanklin hadn't been entirely truthful with Chief Curry. While Oswald wasn't kept under surveillance, the FBI had been very interested in locating him, particularly after they learned in October that he'd visited the Soviet embassy in Mexico City.

But Curry kept his word. As the chief returned to Captain John—known as Will, his middle name—Fritz's office in Homicide and Robbery a few minutes later, he told the big crowd of reporters, "I do not know if and when the bureau interviewed him [Oswald]."

Our story of Jack Revill's memo and Joe Hosty's remarks must have stung sharply over at the *Times Herald*, for the paper promptly published a poorly considered response that caused embarrassment even to some of its own reporters. The afternoon our story ran, the *Times Herald* bannered its front page with "FBI Denies Statement on Oswald," and quoted Hoover directly. Referring to Revill's recollection, the director allegedly said, "That is absolutely false. The agent made no such statement, and the FBI had no such knowledge."

It was a great knock-down of our original story, except for one problem—the Hoover quote was a fabrication. My source for this information was the article's putative writer, George Carter. Angry and deeply embarrassed, George called me to say that not only was his name put on the story without his knowledge but also that the Hoover interview had never occurred. The FBI director would not talk to the *Times Herald*, Carter told me. He wasn't sure whether the newspaper blithely spliced his name to another official's words or, even worse, made up the quotes altogether.

The controversy over Agent Hosty's remark to Lieutenant Revill wasn't the only negative fallout for the bureau in the aftermath of the Kennedy assassination. There were other FBI shenanigans going on as well—a cover-up, if you will, that I helped to illuminate a dozen years later.

In 1975, I was working for my former competitor, the *Times Herald*, when my publisher, Tom Johnson, walked into my office with eyes as big as saucers. "I've got the biggest story you ever heard of," he said. "It's about Oswald." Tom said he'd learned from a highly reliable source the previous night that just a few days before the assassination, an irate Oswald visited the local FBI office and left a threatening note for Hosty. As Johnson heard the story, Oswald threatened to kill Hosty or to blow up the FBI offices.

Johnson had given his word not to reveal his source, and I was frankly dubious about the story. By 1975, I'd run down dozens of equally tantalizing, but invariably false, self-aggrandizing tales spun by people supposedly in a position to know. Nevertheless my investigative partner Bob Dudney and I were assigned to check it out. Since I knew the event Johnson had attended, I scanned the guest list for possible leads. Sure enough, two FBI agents had been at the dinner as well. One, I knew, was an information sieve. The other wouldn't share such a secret with his mother on her deathbed.

With the help of the tenacious Dudney, I dug through every source we could think of and discovered, by golly, Johnson was right. On August 31, under the page one headline "Oswald Threat Revealed," we published a package of stories that publicly disclosed the note's existence for the first time. The stories explained how it had possibly been kept secret even from FBI headquarters and that it had been deliberately destroyed by Hosty shortly after the assassination.

"I am worried it will further damage the FBI," a confidential source inside the bureau told us. "It was a bureaucratic screw-up. Nobody did the follow-up on it, and the letter was destroyed. They didn't want anyone to know that Oswald had come by the offices, that he had left a threat, that we had failed to put him under surveillance."

This is how it occurred: Ten days before the assassination, after learning from Marina that an FBI agent twice had been out to the Paine house on Fifth Street in Irving, Oswald went to the Dallas FBI office in search of Hosty. Informed that the agent was not in, Oswald handed receptionist Nannie Lee Fenner an unsealed envelope, asked her to give it to Hosty, and departed.

As Hosty later recalled in his memoir, *Assignment Oswald*, "It said, in effect, 'If you want to talk to me, you should talk to me to my face. Stop harassing my wife, and stop trying to ask her about me. You have no right to harass her.'" According to Hosty, the note was unsigned. Others who read it say otherwise. Not only did Oswald sign it, they told us, but in it he directly threatened to blow up the FBI office. The note did not mention President Kennedy.

Fenner read the note and showed it to Kyle Clark, assistant special agent in charge, who also read it and instructed the receptionist to place it in Joe Hosty's mail box. Hosty reported that he filed away the note after reading it and thought no more of the matter at the time.

Our *Times Herald* stories caused quite a stir, leading to an internal FBI investigation and congressional hearings in October. That month, FBI Deputy Associate Director James B. Adams told a House Judiciary subcommittee that Hosty remembered destroying the note but claimed he did so under orders from Gordon Shanklin, who had twice directly denied to Dudney and me that he knew anything about the note.

In Hosty's version of the events, Shanklin confronted him with the letter on the night of November 22. "What the hell is this?" he recalled Shanklin saying. "It's no big deal," Hosty replied. "Just your typical guff."

Shanklin was apoplectic. "What do you mean, 'typical guff'? This note was written by Oswald, the probable assassin of the president, and Oswald brought the note into this office just ten days ago! What the hell do you think Hoover's going to do if he finds out about this note?"

According to Hosty, when Shanklin calmed down, he ordered the agent to compose a memo that explained the circumstances of the letter. Two days later, following Oswald's murder by Jack Ruby, Hosty was summoned once more into Shanklin's office.

Shanklin, a chain smoker, put a lit cigarette in his ashtray and stood up behind his desk to speak. "Joe," Hosty remembers him saying, "Now that Oswald is dead, there clearly isn't going to be a trial." Hosty watched as Shanklin reached into his desk drawer, produced the Oswald note together with the agent's Friday night memo, handed them both to Hosty and said, "Here, take these. I don't want to ever see them again." Hosty says he began tearing up the papers there in Shanklin's office.

"No! Not here!" said Shanklin. "I told you I don't want to see them again. Now get them out of here."

So, Joe Hosty walked down to the men's room, which was empty, and headed for the first stall, where he tore the papers into little shreds and flushed them down the toilet. Down the drain, I thought, literally. I hoped the cliché didn't turn out to be prophetic.

J. Edgar Hoover, who died in 1972, probably did find out about the Oswald letter, according to his former number three man at the bureau, William C. Sullivan, whom we reached at his New Hampshire retirement home in 1975. Sullivan pointed out to us that Hosty was suspended for thirty days and then given a disciplinary transfer to the Kansas City office after the Warren Commission finished its work in the autumn of 1964. Hoover, Sullivan explained, "was responsible for the transfer. Somebody must have discussed something with him, or Hosty wouldn't have been transferred."

When Hosty later called me, he told a different version of what occurred. He said he'd rifled a safe in the FBI's Kansas City office and discovered there that some of his reports had been altered to justify his suspension and transfer. He also believed he knew how Dudney and I had learned of the Oswald letter's destruction and began to repeat the story as he related it in *Assignment Oswald*. I cut him off.

"Yes, I said, "I read your book, and you said that Bob Dudney overheard that at a party a fraternity brother had invited him to in Dallas. That isn't how we learned of that at all. You apparently don't have the slightest idea who revealed that."

"Well, it doesn't matter," Hosty replied defensively. "The damage was done."

Gordon Shanklin, now deceased, retired in 1975, insisting to the end that he knew nothing about the Oswald visit or letter even though Bob Dudney's later review of the Justice Department's assassination files revealed that a dozen or more employees of the Dallas FBI office knew of the assassin's visit. In September 2003, the newly built FBI offices in Dallas were officially named the J. Gordon Shanklin Building.

CHAPTER FOUR

The First Conspiracy Theorist: Mr. Stalls

Within a couple of hours of Oswald's arrest, I came up with several possible Oak Cliff addresses for him, plus a couple of other names to check out, along with an alias, Alek Hidell. I can't recall how I got this information—it's possible that Jim Ewell or Harry McCormick or some other reporter gave it to me—but the original source was the wallet Oswald carried that day.

I headed out in my 1961 Ford Fairlane, little realizing how strange and convoluted a journey I was embarked upon. For the great majority of reporters in Dallas that day, the Kennedy assassination would be an intense but brief brush with history. That certainly would have been my expectation, had anyone asked. But for reasons I cannot fully explain, the story grabbed me and wouldn't let go. Part of the reason was sheer coincidence and dumb luck. I was at the right places at the right times. As the saga unfolded, I picked up threads that were impossible to put down.

As other reporters returned to their routines, almost by default I became the guy at the *News*, and then other news organizations, who looked into new leads as well as the bogus assertions of the countless nuts and fakes irresistibly drawn to the Kennedy assassination. I met a lot of very unusual people and heard a number of bizarre stories. In time, I also grew weary of it all.

On day one, though, I was energized. At thirty-two years old, I had been a professional newspaperman since my mid-teens, working at papers in my home state, West Virginia, then Arkansas, Kansas, and Texas as well as United Press International in Denver. I'd covered everything from high school sports to tornadoes, statewide political races, rapes, murders, and space travel but clearly nothing so cataclysmic as a presidential assassination.

After witnessing Oswald's arrest, I began checking out the addresses on my list. The first one was an apartment building. There was no sign that Oswald had ever lived there. I asked around the neighborhood. "Do you know Alek Hidell or Lee Harvey Oswald?"

Nothing.

So I moved on to the second address, a little house where I could hear music and voices from within. I knocked on the door and waited and waited and knocked again. No answer. So I knocked once more, and a very large Hispanic male opened the door with a scowl. He was completely nude as was the female I saw dashing toward a bathroom behind him.

"Do you know Lee Harvey Oswald?" I asked, possibly the most pointless question of my entire career. I might was well have tried to sell him a set of encyclopedias. "No, no, no," the man replied in a manner that strongly discouraged further discourse.

"Well, thank you," I answered, backing steadily away. "I'm sure I can find somebody, uh . . . "

The third address was the charm. Earlene Roberts, the house-keeper, greeted me at the door of the rooming house at 1026 North Beckley. Peering from behind thick eyeglasses, Mrs. Roberts told me that I was the first reporter on the scene. The police and federal agents had just left after thoroughly searching the place.

She said she knew Mr. Oswald as Mr. Lee, a quiet loner who'd rented a room for eight dollars a week since October 14. She even offered to give me the rooming house register, a loose-leaf notebook in which Oswald had printed the name O. H. Lee. Like a fool, I declined.

Mr. Lee had suddenly appeared about one o'clock that afternoon. "He came in running like the dickens," she said, and didn't respond when she asked him his hurry. "[He] just ran in his room, got a short tan coat, and ran back out."

Lee Harvey Oswald had also picked up the .38 revolver with which he'd soon murder Officer Tippit.

Inside Mrs. Roberts showed me the spare, eight-by-eleven, first-floor room that Oswald had occupied over the past several weeks. There wasn't much to see—no personal items, nothing on the walls, just some cheap furniture, a torn-up bed, and a banana peel discarded in the waste basket. Mr. Lee was very neat and clean, she said, ate a lot of fruit, and made himself coffee and sandwiches in his tiny room. He also kept early hours.

"He was always in bed by 9:30 or 10:00 p.m.," said Mrs. A. C. Johnson, Oswald's landlady, who walked in with her husband as I was speaking to the housekeeper. Mr. Johnson recollected that Mr. Lee liked to listen to the radio.

"He was always very quiet and polite," Mrs. Roberts added, but kept to himself, rarely mixed with the other roomers, and never received visitors.

He did use the telephone quite a lot, Mr. Johnson said, and frequently called a prefix in the Dallas suburb of Irving. (I never figured out how he knew that since it was not a long distance call.) Oswald always spoke on the phone "in that foreign language," he said—Russian—easily heard but indecipherable by other roomers watching television nearby.

On my second return to the newsroom, Harry McCormick called the city desk from City Hall to report that the cops were questioning someone who apparently knew Oswald. Harry's call was forwarded to my desk about seven o'clock. "I don't know what role he plays," McCormick told me. "But I looked through Captain Fritz's office window, and he's sitting there wearing some kind of uniform. He doesn't look angry or scared, seems to be laughing and chatting amiably."

Thanks to Harry's tip, we sent a photographer down to get a picture of the mystery witness. I was planning to go snoop around Captain Fritz's office, too, when Johnny King came by my desk. The city editor wanted to know if I'd written up everything I'd reported in Oak Cliff that day.

When I said I had, he indicated my next assignment would be to find H. L. Hunt and General Walker. "Find out where they were today and what they're saying—" King began. Then he broke off and said, "Oh, wait a minute. We haven't anything from the Tippit family. We know hardly anything about them. Run on out there and see what you can come up with. I'll handle the Hunt angle."

This was not a plum assignment. As I mentioned, cop killings are always big news whenever they occur. They tend to put the fallen officer's comrades in an angry, vengeful mood. Reporters often bear the brunt of this hostility.

In those days, most city editors had just the reporter for such stories, some crusty old veteran totally indifferent to what the dead policeman's colleagues and family thought or felt. He'd go to the victim's house, write down the hot quotes, even steal a picture if need be.

Fortunately I had not been used in that manner in recent years.

"Oh my God!" said McCormick when I told him by phone where I was headed instead of City Hall. "They're making you do that?"

Then he considered his own situation. Harry was a dogged police reporter, but he was not bull dogged. In his sixties by then and a dapper dresser, he did not revel in the bedlam engulfing City Hall. Looking out the window of the Burglary and Theft Bureau, he said he saw at least eighty wild-eyed reporters battling for position on the third-floor corridor, clamoring for comment from the police, witnesses, and even Lee Harvey Oswald himself, who was being held in a high-security cell on the fifth floor. "They're like a pack of wild dogs," McCormick said.

When I arrived at the Tippit house, there were cars, pickups, and police cruisers lined up in each direction. I was not about to approach Tippit's shocked and grieving wife, Marie, or any other member of the family for comment. But I couldn't go back to the newsroom with nothing, so I gleaned what comment I could from the gathered police officers, including Bill Anglin, who was kind enough to talk to me for a few minutes.

I returned for a third time to the *News*, typed up my notes, and finally headed home. It was about ten o'clock. What a strange day, I thought as I drove.

Little did I know it was about to get a bit stranger.

* * *

My wife and I lived in what a $9,000-per-year newspaper reporter could afford in those days, a tiny, one-bedroom apartment on Belmont Street in East Dallas, a couple of miles from downtown. As I approached our building, I found an odd, bedraggled little man sitting on my doorstep. He was wearing an overcoat despite the mildness of the evening.

My wife whispered to me that she hadn't known what to do with him. "He almost cried when I told him he couldn't wait for you," she explained. "So I said, 'Sit down here, and you'll see him when he arrives.' I told him you might be late."

The little man introduced himself as Rodney Stalls and told me that until recently he'd worked as an engineer at one of the many electronics and aeronautical companies in and near Dallas. I couldn't imagine what Mr. Stalls wanted with me at that hour until he began to spin a conspiracy theory of the day's shootings, the first of hundreds I'd eventually hear.

I moved him away from my door and over to the stairwell.

"It's the Russians and H. L. Hunt," he began. "I've been getting messages about it for weeks now."

New to such thinking, I made the mistake of trying to reason with my visitor. The Russians very possibly were mixed up in the assassination, I agreed, but not in league with H. L. Hunt, who feared and hated commies as intensely as anyone I'd ever encountered.

"Listen!" Stalls interrupted me. "I know what I'm talking about." His voice began to rise, and his tone turned urgent. "It was Hunt who caused me to get fired because I knew what the Russians were planning and tried to convince my bosses."

Stalls was clearly troubled, but was he a complete nut? I knew I'd better make sure, so I asked if he had any evidence. Immediately he produced from beneath his heavy coat a fat sheaf of yellowed and well-thumbed pages and handed them to me. I spent half an hour plowing through the mess. There was no mention of Oswald, Dallas, Kennedy, or assassination anywhere in them, just a lot of gibberish. So now I needed an exit strategy.

"May I copy these?" I asked, "and discuss them with my editor?"

"Absolutely not," he answered. "If you don't trust me with all that I have shown you, then I must look for an honest reporter, one who will listen."

This is what I hoped he'd say. Stalls explained that I wasn't his first choice in any event. That person was Bob Fenley at the *Times Herald*. He said he'd tried to reach Fenley at the paper, but "obviously they got to him. He's not even in the phone book anymore. Do you know him? I saw his name on a story yesterday, but they wouldn't give me his home number at the *Times Herald*. I'll bet he would listen to me."

"Of course, I know Bob," I said as a realization dawned. "He and I cover science and aerospace together." I'd wondered how Stalls connected me to the assassination. My stories on the assassination and the Tippit killing hadn't even appeared in the paper yet. Of course, he'd sought out Bob and me because we covered stories of professional interest to him. Stalls hauled out an envelope with the name Bob Finley written on it. This accounted for his trouble with the phone book. He'd misspelled Bob's name.

Then an insidious idea occurred to me. "I'm sure Bob would be pleased to talk to you," I said, and informed Mr. Stalls that I'd seen Fenley just that day, that he looked very well indeed, and I was certain "nobody had gotten to him." To help him along even further, I corrected his spelling.

My wife at last rescued me with a call to dinner, a blessing because I had no desire to hurt or further upset my zany visitor. Stalls quickly rolled his papers under his arm and pleasantly made his exit.

I never saw him again and, of course, was afraid to mention Stalls to Fenley. About three years later, however, at a Dallas Press Club committee meeting, I asked Bob if he remembered talking to an ex-engineer about H. L. Hunt and the Kennedy assassination.

"Oh, that," he laughed. "I knew you sent him to me. He told me that you were too inexperienced to handle it and that you'd recommended that he approach me. Thanks. And by the way, how do you know I haven't sent some weirdos to you too?"

He didn't have to. There were plenty to go around.

CHAPTER FIVE

Oswald's Convoluted Escape Route

I n the early hours after Oswald's arrest, a question foremost in many people's minds was how he'd pulled off such an audacious crime. People especially wanted to know how he'd slipped out of the book depository so quickly and made his way back to Oak Cliff. He seemed like a phantom.

Friday afternoon in the newsroom, after I returned from Oswald's boarding house, Larry Grove repeatedly asked me what I knew about Oswald's escape. At the time, my answer was, "Nothing." But I agreed with Larry that we needed to nail that down.

We quickly learned that Oswald normally spent Monday through Thursday nights at 1026 North Beckley. On Fridays, his book depository co-worker, Buell Wesley Frazier, drove him out to Mrs. Paine's house in Irving for the weekend. Frazier, who lived very near Ruth Paine, then drove Oswald back into Dallas on Monday mornings to begin the depository workday at half past eight.

The Thursday evening before the assassination, Oswald varied his routine. Instead of returning as usual to his boarding house, he rode out to Irving with Frazier, played for a while with June Lee, ate an early dinner with Marina and Mrs. Paine, and turned in at nine.

When he arose the next morning, Marina was still asleep. Oswald slipped off his wedding ring and placed it on the dresser next to his wallet, which contained $170. When he was arrested several hours later, he had $13.87 in cash on him.

As Buell Frazier was finishing his breakfast that morning, his sister Linnie Mae Randle saw Oswald walking toward Buell's car carrying what she described as a "heavy brown bag," which he placed on the rear seat.

As he walked with Oswald from his back door to the car, Buell Frazier asked, "What's the package, Lee?"

"Curtain rods," Oswald answered. Frazier also noticed his co-worker wasn't carrying a sack lunch as usual. Oswald said he planned to buy lunch that day.

The two men arrived for work at the depository on time. Oswald's lunch break was supposed to last forty-five minutes, but because time clocks weren't used at the depository, it isn't possible to pin when or if he broke for lunch.

He shot the president at 12:30, then stashed the Mannlicher-Carcano, and headed downstairs where he encountered Dallas Police Officer Marrion Baker, who jumped off his motorcycle and ran inside the book depository with Roy Truly, the building superintendent. Baker poked his sidearm in Oswald's stomach as he asked Truly, "Do you know this man? Does he work here?" Truly said Oswald did, and Baker let him go.

"Oswald looked a bit startled," the superintendent would recall, "as you or I would if someone threw a gun on you. But he didn't appear too nervous or panicky."

Moments later, Oswald showed radio executive Pierce Allman where the phone booths were as he departed the building. He was clear of the depository by 12:32, or about the time I had my makeshift reporting tools assembled and went to work interviewing. This is where the trail went cold.

Larry and I began retracing his escape route by interviewing everybody we could think of at the depository, the sheriff's office, the police department, federal law enforcement agencies, the DA's office, even some criminal lawyers we knew.

Nothing.

"Hell of a lot easier writing a column," Grove said in discouragement. "Do you do this kind of stuff all the time?"

Then we caught a break. Somehow I ascertained that the mystery man we had photographed at police headquarters on Friday evening was a bus driver named Cecil J. McWatters. I had photographs, but there was a hitch. Jack Beers, the *News* photographer, had gotten McWatters's image as the witness was being escorted from City Hall. But Beers had also photographed another witness leaving the building, and he didn't know which one was our bus driver.

Larry and I took the two photos with us on Saturday morning when we went downtown to visit the Dallas Transit Company. A supervisor there quickly picked out McWatters, checked the schedule, and said the driver would be back at work on Sunday. Around six o'clock Sunday evening, as McWatters entered the office to check out for the day, we were waiting for him.

An eighteen-year veteran of the transit company, McWatters, known as Mac, remembered that he was steering his white, forty-four-passenger, No. 433 bus west on Elm Street when a traffic snarl brought him to a complete halt near Field Street, a few blocks east of the book depository. It was approximately 12:40.

"That's when I saw him," McWatters recalled as he enjoyed a cigar. "He beat pretty hard on the bus door and I let him in. The fare was twenty-three cents."

Oswald asked McWatters for a transfer and took the second seat behind the driver. Had he remained aboard No. 433, the bus would have taken him directly past the corner of Elm and Houston, where ten minutes before he'd shot and killed President Kennedy. Instead, according to McWatters, as the bus slowed once more in traffic,

Oswald rose abruptly and disembarked at Lamar Street, about half of the way to the book depository.

To McWatters, Lee Harvey Oswald was just another anonymous fare. He was never able to identify Oswald conclusively as the slightly built young man who rode his bus for about five minutes that Friday afternoon.

About five hours later that day, he told us, the police pulled him over near City Hall and took him up to Captain Fritz's office for questioning. Detectives told him they'd found the transfer ticket he'd issued Oswald in the suspect's clothing. It distinctly bore the driver's stamp and was one of only two he gave out all day.

When the Dallas police showed him a lineup, he told officers that Oswald was the right height, weight, and coloring, but he could not be absolutely certain.

"They sure wanted me to pick him out, without reservation," McWatters recalled to us. "I couldn't do that, not for positive."

Like all reporters, I had to hit it very hard sometimes, especially on the science and aviation beat. I covered all manned space activities for the paper, which meant dealing with NASA, a notoriously and annoyingly secretive government organization. On the aviation side, many of the really important stories were about mistakes and malfunctions—crashes and casualties—which required a lot of digging as well as assiduous cultivation of sources. Now, some of that hard work was going to pay off in an entirely unforeseeable way. I received a telephone call from a source I'd met at lunch the previous year with Lieutenant Colonel John A. "Shorty" Powers, the famous onetime pilot and public affairs officer for NASA's original Mercury Program and the man who coined the term, *a-ok*.

"I live just a few houses from a guy who says he carried Oswald in his cab on Friday," the source told me. "I knew you'd know if he's lying or not."

Wow! Could this be real? Excited, I asked my new best friend for the cab driver's name and address and said I'd check it out.

"William Whaley," he said, and gave me an address in Lewisville, a little town about twenty-five miles northwest of Dallas. I grabbed Grove and off we went.

I hadn't risked telephoning Whaley in advance. If the cab driver didn't feel like talking, it would be much easier for him to hang up the telephone than to banish my smiling face from his front door. I did call Whaley's employer to see if he was working that day. I was told the cab driver's wife was ill and that he'd taken the day off to be with her. That explained why no one was home when we reached the Whaley address.

Larry and I drove around the neighborhood for a while, stopped for lunch at a decent barbecue spot, and then returned to the still-empty house. We spotted a woman entering the residence next door. She told us that Mrs. Whaley was at Flow Hospital in Denton, another eighteen miles out, and that her husband probably was there with her.

So Larry and I rushed to Flow Hospital, where Whaley's wife indeed was a patient. She was asleep, we were told, and couldn't be disturbed. Several people had helpful guesses where her husband might be—the cafeteria, a convenience store down the street—but none panned out.

Back to Lewisville.

Mr. Whaley hadn't returned home, so I asked his neighbor what make and model of car he drove, thinking we might start checking the streets and lots surrounding Flow Hospital.

"Oh, he drives his cab," she said.

Larry and I exchanged a glance, feeling more than a little foolish, and thanked her.

Spotting his cab shouldn't be too tough, I thought, as we returned once again to Denton.

By now it was late afternoon. Whaley was not inside the hospital, and his yellow cab was not parked in any hospital lot. Just as I was about to take the Lord's name in vain, Larry grinned and said, "Hey, big Hugh, look over there," and he pointed at a yellow cab, apparently empty, parked about a block away, easily in sight of the hospital doors.

I'd never make a good repo man.

We both ran to the cab, thinking we finally had Mr. Whaley cornered—sort of. He had to return to his car at some time. As it turned out, we didn't have to wait. Drawing closer to the vehicle, we saw a pair of legs dangling out one window. Attached to them was our quarry, sound asleep in his 1961 Checker.

We awakened him, gently, and introduced ourselves. William Wayne Whaley, known as Chief, said police detectives had been all over him since the assassination and that he needed some time for himself and for his sick wife. His boss had told him to take the day off, which he had.

We proceeded slowly. Whaley laughed to hear of our adventures in search of him. He and Larry hit it off right away, especially when they discovered they had both served in the South Pacific during World War II. Whaley had been a Navy gunner and won a Navy Cross over Iwo Jima, he said. I was far too young to know anything about that.

Reporters sometimes forget the objective of any interview is to extract information. In this case, Larry was connecting with Whaley better than I, so he led the discussion. They talked about Mrs. Whaley's condition. They reminisced about the war. They even discussed the pros and cons of working for a cab company. Chief Whaley said he had put in thirty-seven years behind the wheel, making him the senior driver at the company.

At last, we settled down to discuss Oswald. Whaley recollected that he'd dropped off a fifty-five cent fare at the Dallas Greyhound Bus Terminal on the corner of Lamar and Commerce sometime before noon and was about to go inside to buy a pack of cigarettes when he saw a young man walking south on Lamar, approximately three blocks from where Oswald had departed McWatters's city bus. He was waving at Whaley, trying to get his attention.

"He was very polite," according to Whaley. "Said something like 'May I have the cab, sir?' I told him, 'You sure can. Get in!'" Oswald climbed in the front seat.

"No sooner had he closed the door," Whaley continued, "when an old lady stuck her head through the window on his side and said, 'Driver, can you get me a cab down here? I've been waiting . . .'"

"I guess I hadn't seen her in the doorway, and here he came walking. He opened his door a bit like he was going to get out, and he told her, 'Here, I'll let you have this one.' She said, 'No, that's all right. He can get me another one.' So he settled back, looked at me, and said, '500 North Beckley.'"

Sirens were screaming all over the area, Whaley said, "and I couldn't figure out why. Police cruisers were crisscrossing, making U-turns, then screeching off. I remember saying to him, 'What the hell's going on? I wonder what's happening.'"

The young man looked at the cab driver but didn't answer. "I just thought to myself, here's a guy who wants to be left alone," Whaley remembered. "So I left him alone."

Their route took them directly past 1026 N. Beckley and five blocks further on, where the man gave Whaley a dollar for the ninety-five-cent ride.

"I pulled over to the curb and he got out, didn't say anything else," Whaley said.

What about the tip, we asked.

"Well, if you can call a nickel a tip, I guess he did."

According to the cab driver's logbook, he most likely picked up the fare at approximately quarter to one and delivered him to his destination in Oak Cliff about ten minutes later.

Whaley was unaware he'd driven Lee Harvey Oswald's getaway car until the next morning when he saw Oswald's picture in the *News*. He told his boss about it, and within twenty minutes, he was on his way to a line-up, where he picked Oswald from among five or six other men.

CHAPTER SIX

TV News Comes into Its Own

The Kennedy assassination was a watershed event for journalism. Up to then, television news was mostly a novelty. The era of the celebrity network anchor supplanting a kid on a bike as bearer of the evening news was not yet born. The reflex habit of tuning to cable television to follow any breaking story was still decades away. Daily newspapers were the most common, and most trusted, source of news in the country.

But November 22, 1963, went far to change all that even if television coverage of the event and its immediate aftermath in Dallas was spotty and amateurish by today's standards. Only Abraham Zapruder, a local purveyor of women's fashions, caught the assassination itself on film, using his 8 mm Bell & Howell home movie camera.

The most vivid images of the weekend, in my view, were Jack Beers' great picture showing Ruby moving toward Oswald and the even greater Pulitzer Prize-winning still of the actual murder, taken by *Times Herald* photographer Bob Jackson.

At its best, however, the television coverage, particularly of Oswald's murder, was more immediate and dramatic than anything you could put in a newspaper column.

A revolution had begun.

The first victims of television's newly discovered power to cover breaking stories would be the afternoon dailies. Yet on November 22 in Dallas, it was the afternoon paper, the *Times Herald*, which scored a lot of the early newsbreaks. The reason was simple. With an early afternoon copy deadline already in place, and much of the boilerplate reporting in hand, the paper could instantly mobilize. The *Times Herald* got a special edition with a 150-point banner proclaiming PRESIDENT DEAD. It was on the street by half past two that afternoon. The frightened, jittery Dallas citizenry, hungry for any information, paid as much as a dollar apiece for the nickel newspapers, a circulation manager's dream.

Across the way in Fort Worth, the *Star-Telegram* began cranking out serial editions of its afternoon paper, remaking page one over and over as more news broke and Fort Worth readers lined up around the block to purchase the paper.

The *News* hit the streets overnight with a two-line banner:

KENNEDY SLAIN

ON DALLAS STREET

We produced what I think was a comprehensive and balanced twelve pages of coverage devoted to the assassination, including everything from a long Kennedy obituary to wire service reports from around the world to my interviews with Nick McDonald, Earlene Roberts, and others.

The centerpiece was a long narrative crafted from staff feeds by Paul Crume, the best front-page columnist working west of the Mississippi at the time. He was drafted into acting as a sort of super rewrite man that day. Johnny King later told me that Crume filled three waste baskets with wadded balls of discarded copy as he labored over his typewriter to create the most seamless story possible.

Unfortunately two major errors crept into the piece. One, that Oswald's assassination weapon was a 6.5 Mauser rifle (not a Mannlicher-Carcano) and two, that Kennedy died in surgery on the sixth floor of Parkland Hospital instead of where he actually expired, Trauma Room No.1, on the ground floor. Both mistakes were soon twisted to the many uses of conspiracy buffs. Among the most persistent fictions to emerge from the second error is that the president really didn't die that day but survived and was placed on life support systems in a persistent vegetative state on Parkland's sixth floor.

Never mind that Parkland had no sixth floor. The story never went away.

Far less excusable were the multiple mistakes that United Press International White House correspondent Albert Merriman Smith wove into his spot news account of the assassination. The fifty-year-old Smith, who used his middle name, Merriman, was riding in the front seat of the press car, six vehicles behind the presidential limousine, when the shooting started. At his feet, beneath the dash board, was a radiophone, installed for the use of all five reporters in the car.

The UPI man grabbed the phone at once and dictated his lead—"Three shots were fired at President Kennedy's motorcade in downtown Dallas today"—but then refused to give up the phone to his archrival in the back seat, Jack Bell of the Associated Press.

Bob Baskin, my *News* colleague who also was in the car, later recalled, "I thought Jack was going to kill Smitty. He was leaning over the seat, flailing at him, screaming, 'Gimme the phone! Gimme the phone!' But he couldn't get it. Smith crawled up partially under the dashboard. It wasn't a pretty scene."

Smith may have gotten the story first, but he got a lot of it wrong, committing two major errors in his first five paragraphs. He erroneously reported that Governor Connally had been hit in the head and that the assassination weapon was an automatic. In a later version of his wire story, Smith also mistakenly reported that the president had been hit in the right temple and that a Mauser, not the Mannlicher-Carcano, had been recovered on the fifth, not the sixth, floor of the book depository.

He nonetheless was later honored, as his Pulitzer citation read, "For his outstanding coverage of the assassination of President Kennedy."

Getting the facts wrong wasn't the press's only shortcoming in the hours immediately following the assassination.

Painful as such screw-ups were, they were mistakes of inadvertence—Paul didn't mean to get it wrong. Not so the *News* editorial that day, a noxious blend of sanctimony and disingenuousness. Calling the assassination a "shameful mark on this city's history," the writer loftily continued, "We join the rest of the nation in heartfelt sympathy and trust that the warped and distorted who become unstable in their opposition will retreat into darkness and not emerge until they regain the light of reasonableness and balance."

The *News* editorialist seemed almost gleeful the following day for the chance to blame communists for Kennedy's death. "In the first agonizing hours after the assassination of President Kennedy," the editorial began, "the assumption was made by many and openly expressed by a few that the blame for this hideous crime rested at the doorstep of the 'radical right' in Dallas. Quite the opposite seems to be the case, making these assumptions and charges unfair. The man charged with the murder is pro-communist with strong 'radical left' ties."

The piece went on, "We have seen once again the murderous demonstration that the size of the domestic communist force is not the issue. Numbers mean very little in a conspiracy. Too many have scoffed at the danger by insisting that we have a mere 'handful' of domestic Reds—forgetting that a single determined procommunist can murder the President of the United States and plunge an entire nation into serious crisis."

Relying on pitifully weak evidence to elevate a jackleg Marxist such as Lee Harvey Oswald to membership in the supposed international communist conspiracy was precisely the sort of irresponsible straw man fabrication at which the *News* editorial writers excelled. No self-respecting communist would have wanted himself or his movement associated with the likes of Oswald.

Behind the *News* editorial's bluster, however, lurked a different truth. It wasn't political conservatism but intolerance—outright knee-jerk hostility to any opposing view—that characterized the thought of Ted Dealey and his fellow believers on the right. It was this brand of extremism that was discredited in Dallas by the events of November 22.

Fear for their own safety gripped some of the anticommunist crusaders after the shootings, possibly for good reason. Larry Schmidt and Bernard Weissman left town, the dust of the American Fact-Finding Committee settling to earth in their wake. General Walker grabbed a plane for Shreveport, Louisiana, where he hunkered down for several days.

H. L. Hunt's daughter, Margaret Hunt Hill, later wrote that the Dallas police advised her father to decamp for safer precincts. "I do not get along well with being scared," the old man replied. "I am safe in my home."

Then the FBI called, "and warned him," Ms. Hill reported, "that mobs were singling out all conservatives who had been vocally anti-Kennedy as Daddy had been in his radio broadcasts." H. L. departed Dallas "within hours," she wrote.

The Hunt family went on high alert. "We feared for anyone named Hunt," she recalled. "It was traumatic for the family to wonder if somebody was going to seek us out in revenge. In lock step, the media adhered to the story that Daddy had created an atmosphere of hate around Dallas toward Kennedy. It lasted two or three weeks. There were no attempts though we did receive some hostile phone calls and a lot of hate mail, which naturally caused concern."

A more measured view of the assassination and its impact on Dallas came from Stanley Marcus, whom I interviewed in 1973 for a tenth-anniversary assassination retrospective in *Newsweek*. Marcus was a marketing genius who transformed the store his father and aunt founded in Dallas in 1907 into a high-end retailing juggernaut. He was internationally respected as president of Neiman Marcus and a preeminent local arbiter of taste. More important, his voice counted among members of the Citizens Council, wealthy Anglo-Christian oligarchs who then controlled every aspect of municipal affairs in Dallas.

I asked Marcus how a liberal Jew could flourish so in mid-century Dallas.

"The fact that I've been successful economically," he answered, gave him legitimacy in the Dallas business community. "If I hadn't been successful economically, I'd have gotten the boot."

Marcus never shied from the fray. When it was announced in early October 1963 that Ambassador Adlai Stevenson would come to town on the twenty-fourth to address a UN Day celebration at the Memorial Theater, General Walker immediately booked the facility for a "U.S. Day" rally on the twenty-third and even prevailed on Governor Connally to proclaim October 23, 1963, as U.S. Day in Texas. Walker's event drew approximately twelve hundred hard-right loyalists whom the general inflamed with his rhetoric.

The UN Day organizers, led by local businessman Jack Goren, knew to expect trouble the next night after Walker practically equated attendance at the Stevenson rally with being a communist. Worried about Stevenson's safety, Goren secured a promise from Chief Curry for added police security on the twenty-fourth. Stanley Marcus accompanied Ambassador Stevenson to the meeting and introduced him to the large crowd. "Dallas was festering," Marcus remembered. "There was tension, hate, and extreme bigotry."

The pickets who greeted Stevenson and Marcus outside the hall were noisy yet civil for the most part. But inside, as Stevenson began to speak, "there were hisses and grumbles, and finally we thought we should end it and get out of there," said Marcus.

As they hurried to their car, placard-waving protestors chanted "U.S., not the UN! U.S., not the UN!" A young student spat on the ambassador. When Stevenson broke from his police cordon to ask one woman politely why she was screaming at him, she hit him with her sign.

Once safely in the limo, Marcus recalled, Stevenson "was white as a sheet. His eyes bulged out. He said he couldn't understand this, not in America. He said he had been involved in many situations where pickets or opponents were present but that this was different."

As the ambassador wiped away the spittle with his handkerchief, he turned to Marcus and wondered, "Are these people, or are they animals?"

Mayor Earle Cabell and the Dallas City Council apologized to Stevenson and made it a crime in the city to curse or to shout obscenities during a public event. Congressman Alger thought that was overdoing things. He later said the boy who spat at the ambassador simply "lost his head because of his resentment against the UN that threatens his freedom and his country's freedom."

"I was physically afraid," Marcus told me. "I never want to go through anything like that again."

Yet he didn't back down. On New Year's Day, 1964, Marcus bought half a page in the *News* and the *Times Herald* for an open letter to the city, titled "What's Right With Dallas?" The letter began by praising the city. "We think that our citizens are friendly and kind-hearted human beings who extend genuinely warm welcomes to newcomers to our city," Marcus wrote. Then he shifted gears: "That doesn't mean there aren't things about Dallas that couldn't be improved."

Turning to his real theme, Marcus denounced political extremists. "The rejection of this spirit of 'absolutism,'" he wrote, "and the acceptance and insistence by all citizens on toleration of differing points of view seem to us to be essential for the future health of our community."

And he took a dig at the *News*. "We believe our newspapers have an important contribution to make in regard to this matter, and we hope they will lead the way by the presentation of balanced points of view on controversial issues." Stanley Marcus took a lot of pride in his letter. "I think [it] contributed to sobering the community," he told me. "I think it helped put things in perspective.

"The community as a whole appreciated the stance on that. But the fact was that we gave them hell without saying so. If we had said, 'What's Wrong With Dallas?' the bricks would have fallen down on me. But by saying, 'What's Right With Dallas?'—leading off with the positive and ending up with the negative—we got the message across in a sugar-coated form."

The ad prompted a rash of credit account cancellations at Neiman Marcus, particularly from hard-right conservatives in the West Texas oil towns of Midland and Odessa. "Obviously some preacher out there was dictating a letter because they were all the same," Marcus recollected. "They were saying I was a radical and had supported a man opposed to the free-enterprise system. They were going to close their accounts.

"I wrote back to answer each, thanking them for writing but telling them that I thought we had one thing in common and that was that we all believed in the democratic way of life and the free-enterprise system. I expressed surprise that, since we believed in the democratic form of government, they would take the role of the dictatorship countries by employing economic sanction.

"I didn't get any answer from most of them, but a couple wrote back and said they hadn't really looked at it that way before and were now sorry that they'd written. Among those who closed their accounts, about 95 percent reopened them within three months."

In all, Marcus believed the assassination was a wake-up call that Dallas generally heeded. "I think the assassination brought about a point where when [Dallas conservatives] started talking about government, you wondered who the monster was that was about to devour you. The federal government was about to devour you. They built it up as a great big monster."

Bruce Alger, adamant as anyone on this point, would lose his congressional seat to Earle Cabell in 1964.

"The assassination sobered the community," said Marcus. "There was recognition of the state of absolutism that had existed, and it gave way to more moderation."

CHAPTER SEVEN

Oswald Arrogant, Defiant

Readers of the Sunday morning *News* were offered two distinct and contrasting views of accused assassin and cop killer Lee Harvey Oswald. "He impressed me as a quiet, rather modest, nice-appearing chap who was doing an extremely good job as far as I could tell," Roy Truly, superintendent at the book depository, told *News* reporter Carlos Conde. "He gave us no trouble, was always on time, and went about his work in such fashion that there was no indication there was anything wrong in his mind."

Directly adjacent to Conde's piece on page ten of the front section, Bill Alexander, assistant district attorney, begged to differ. "He's the most arrogant person I ever met," Alexander told one of our reporters. About seven o'clock on the night of November 22, Alexander represented the State of Texas before Justice of the Peace David L. Johnston at Oswald's arraignment for the murder of Officer J. D. Tippit in Oak Cliff. Before the court proceeding, the assistant DA informed Oswald of the charge in a brief meeting.

"Don't tell me about it," Oswald replied. "Tell my legal representative," even though he had none. In fact, Oswald asked repeatedly to be provided counsel, indicating his choice was either John J. Abt, a New York City attorney associated with left-wing causes, or perhaps a local lawyer from the American Civil Liberties Union. He had applied for membership in the ACLU eighteen days before the assassination. Oswald, in fact, never was provided counsel, which could have caused headaches for the prosecution had he survived to stand trial.

"I got the impression he enjoys being in the spotlight," Alexander said. "It's obvious he is a communist sympathizer."

Oswald apparently disliked Alexander, too. At one point, according to the assistant prosecutor, the accused complained, "The way you're treating me, I might as well be in Russia."

Far trickier than the Tippit indictment would be charging Oswald with assassination. But that was going to be District Attorney Henry Wade's problem.

Henry Wade, Dallas County district attorney from 1951 to 1987, is most widely remembered today as the Wade in *Roe v. Wade*, the 1973 Supreme Court case that made abortion legal in the United States. On November 22, Henry Wade, along with twenty-five hundred others, was just tucking into his steak lunch at the Trade Mart, looking forward to the first couple's imminent arrival, when news of the gunshots in Dealey Plaza reached him and the assembled guests.

Reverend Luther Holcomb, president of the Dallas Ministerial Alliance, led the stunned assemblage in a brief prayer; then Henry Wade headed for his office. "I didn't think I'd be involved in it," Wade later said to me. "About an hour after I got back to the office, I got a call from Barefoot Sanders, the U.S. attorney here. He said, 'Henry, do you realize that the highest federal penalty for killing a president is for assault on a president, and it carries a penalty of just five years? This is going to be your baby.'"

The Justice Department for a time toyed with invoking a federal law against homicides committed on government property—the Lincoln Continental in which Kennedy rode. "It was a possibility," Wade told me, "but they decided it wouldn't cover this case."

Just then, Henry Wade's life was complicated by a radio report that the Dallas police, in a court filing, had somehow implicated the Soviets in Oswald's crimes. Moments later, the district attorney received a call from LBJ aide Cliff Carter in Washington. "He said they were very concerned about how this kind of thing could affect our relations with Russia," Wade recollected. "I was concerned about it, too, because anything you allege in an indictment you have to prove." The DA headed for police headquarters "to make sure they were filing just a straight murder case." Recalling the "wild scene" he encountered, he said, "Newsmen, I would say, created most of it. They were running up and down the hall, trying to get in the room where Oswald was."

He recalled that the evidence against Oswald in the Tippit case was much stronger than for the Kennedy assassination. "The investigators told me that night they had evidence against Oswald that was stronger than it later turned out to be," he said. "They had a palm print on the gun, for example, and an expert who tentatively identified it [as Oswald's]. But I don't think the FBI ever did identify that palm print."

Wade filed his assassination charge against Oswald at approximately half past one in the morning on Saturday, thirteen hours after the crime was committed.

A prosecutor's best evidence usually is a confession, preferably on tape as well as signed. But if ever there was a chance of extracting the truth from Lee Harvey Oswald—a long-shot proposition—the Dallas police fumbled their opportunity.

Captain Will Fritz, 67, a four-decade veteran of the Dallas police force, had been head of the Homicide and Robbery Bureau since the 1930s. Diminutive, low-key, given to mumbling, the captain had a well-deserved reputation as a brilliant interrogator. His forte was putting his subject at ease, developing trust, and then gradually eliciting cooperation. Had Captain Fritz carried out the questioning under rigidly controlled conditions, Oswald might have been coaxed into damning disclosures.

Maybe.

Instead, a stream of cops, federal agents, and assorted law enforcement officials passed in and out of Fritz's office during the Oswald interrogation, including representatives from the FBI, Secret Service, Postal Service, U.S. Marshals, the Dallas police, and the DA's office—even the DA himself. None of the conversations was tape recorded because the Dallas police department lacked the equipment to do so.

To his credit, Captain Fritz understood the importance of creating such a reliable record of interrogations. He had included tape recorders in his budget requests for the past six years, at least, but was always turned down.

In any event, Oswald refused to crack or even bend. If, during approximately eleven hours of intermittent questioning conducted over two days, the prisoner was scared, confused, remorseful, or looking for some sort of deal, he never betrayed it. Instead Oswald remained defiant throughout, by turns sarcastic or silent, apparently energized by this confrontation with authority figures, reveling in their undivided attention, delighting in their frustration.

This was Lee Harvey Oswald's moment.

Fritz later told me that he didn't consider the subject particularly troublesome. "If we would just talk to him quietly," said the captain, "he would respond. But every time I would ask a question that meant something, that would produce evidence, he immediately told me he wouldn't tell me about it. He seemed to anticipate what I was going to ask."

FBI Agent James W. Bookhout, who sat in on much of the interrogation, agreed. "You might say," Bookhout testified before the

Warren Commission, "that any time you asked a question that would be pertinent to the investigation that would be the type of question he would refuse to discuss." Or simply lie about.

For example, Oswald vehemently denied owning a rifle. Even when Captain Fritz showed him a copy of the mail-order invoice that demonstrated he bought the Mannlicher-Carcano under his Alek Hidell alias, he claimed the information was false, that since leaving the Marines, the only thing he'd fired was a little .22.

When detectives H. M. Moore, Gus Rose, and Richard Stovall exercised a search warrant on Saturday morning to examine Oswald's belongings in Ruth Paine's garage, they found two photos. Each clearly depicted him holding a rifle and a pistol. Fritz jammed the pictures at Oswald on Saturday night. "What about these?" the captain asked.

Oswald was not ruffled. "They're obviously fake photographs," he sneered, and cheekily accused the police of superimposing the weapons on pictures taken of him after his arrest. Fritz produced the pictures once again on Sunday morning, but Oswald just laughed and said his nonexistent lawyer would prove they'd been doctored.

The pictures were later authenticated before the Warren Commission by photo experts and by Marina Oswald, who testified that she took the photos herself using Lee's Imperial Reflex camera.

At the initial interrogation, Oswald admitted only to carrying a pistol and resisting arrest. When Fritz asked him why he had a handgun with him in the theater, Oswald replied, "Well, you know about a pistol. I just carried it." He said he bought it in Fort Worth, which the cops already knew to be untrue. The pistol had been mail-ordered from a Los Angeles company.

Asked why he rented the North Beckley Street room under a false name, O. H. Lee, he said the landlady, Mrs. Johnson, just got it mixed up. He insisted he told her he was Lee, not Mr. Lee, even though he'd clearly printed O. H. Lee in the register Earlene Roberts had shown me.

Oswald even lied about his reason for visiting Irving on the night before the assassination. He said he went there on Thursday instead of Friday because Ruth Paine's kids were planning a weekend party. He didn't want to be in the way. There actually was such a party, but it had been held the previous weekend.

Oswald claimed he never mentioned curtain rods to Buell Frazier, adding that Frazier and his sister were both mistaken about him carrying a long package that morning. Oswald said the only sack he carried was his lunch.

He was asked why he left the depository building.

He said foreman Bill Shelley told him there would be no more work, so he left. Shelley later testified he never saw Oswald after noon that day.

The interview sessions were punctuated by two arraignments and three fingerprinting and photographing sessions. Oswald also took part in four line-ups: at 4:35, 6:30, 7:55, and again on Saturday afternoon at 2:15.

Late, about midnight on Friday, as Oswald was being led down the corridor from the final interrogation session of the night, he stopped to hold an impromptu press conference. The brief encounter with reporters was notable on three accounts. First, it was the single time Oswald spoke in public. When a newsman asked if he shot the president, he answered, "No, I have not been charged with that. In fact, nobody has said that to me yet. The first thing I heard about it was when the newspaper reporters in the hall asked me that question."

Second, there was his enigmatic remark to the crowd: "I'm just a patsy." I believe by "patsy" Oswald surely meant to portray himself as an innocent victim of what conspiracy theorist Mark Lane later famously termed the "rush to judgment." The remark has also been interpreted by conspiracy buffs to mean "patsy" in the more specific sense of "fall guy or scapegoat."

Third, there was a surprise presence at the midnight meeting, Jack Ruby. The club owner can be clearly seen in a film record of the session, standing on a table. That an unauthorized civilian at police headquarters should have such casual access to the world's most famous accused killer was just another of the many security screw-ups that characterized the assassination story. This official laxity certainly helped foster some of the darker conspiracy speculation that has hung over Dallas ever since.

At the very least, Chief Jesse Curry emerged from the saga as a well-meaning but weak and ill-prepared administrator whose shortcomings greatly exacerbated a national tragedy. Harsh though fair, in my view, that judgment nevertheless doesn't reach the heart of the matter. Neither the DPD nor the FBI nor even the Secret Service performed as they should have that weekend because no one really believed that such an act against the president was possible, not in the United States.

What we cannot conceive of is impossible to prevent. Stanley Marcus first expressed this insight to me in a different context. "The assassination," he said, "was the beginning of a process that shattered some of the myths about the sanctity of the United States as something God had put on earth that was completely different from any other country. South Americans assassinated their presidents, but in the United States that never happened."

Of course, it did, fairly frequently. Americans just have short memories. Lincoln in 1865. Garfield in 1881. McKinley in 1901. All were cut down. Targets of attempted assassinations include Andrew Jackson, Franklin Roosevelt, Harry Truman, Gerald Ford, and Ronald Reagan. In each case, the assailant acted alone, except for the 1950 attack on Truman, in which two would-be killers took part. Firearms were always the weapon of choice.

Nevertheless, Marcus's point was well taken. "The United States won every war until we got to Vietnam," he continued. "Students never rioted here until the mid-1960s. We've gone through these things ever since, and suddenly Americans have come to realize that the good Lord has not singled them out as a favorite people. America has taken a terrific ego beating, which it well deserved. It was good because we had expanded our ego beyond all sense of objective reality. We now know we are human beings with problems. That should give us a certain degree of humility."

Stanley Marcus died at ninety-six, four months after the events of September 11, 2001.

— ❧ —

Jesse Curry had much to be humble about. Just as the possibility of a Lee Harvey Oswald obviously didn't penetrate too deeply into the federal security agencies' thinking, Curry was blinded by his preconceptions. "We knew some people here were really bitter and wanted Oswald dead," Curry later told me. "That was apparent from the phone calls and just the general mood of the community. But we never, not for a second, thought in terms of just one individual."

The only exception he considered, Curry said, was the possibility of a rogue cop murdering Oswald. "We discussed the fact that some officer might become too emotionally aroused or upset, that he might take things in his own hands," he explained. "That's why we were very careful about those officers we assigned to the basement."

Lee Harvey Oswald was to be taken to the City Hall basement for transfer to veteran Sheriff Bill Decker's custody at the county jail on Dealey Plaza, less than a mile away. The move was anticipated nearly from the moment Oswald was brought to Captain Fritz's office Friday afternoon.

On Saturday afternoon, Dan Rather did a CBS broadcast from the jail, advising viewers that Oswald was expected there "any time now." He described a large wreath of mourning that had been placed on the grassy area just opposite the jail and the book depository. "All day long," said the newsman, "crowds have built up and waned and then again built up as people came by just to look at the spot, walk around the wreath . . . . The crowd now has moved to the sidewalk facing the county jail, facing the wreath. Not many people at this moment are looking at the building where the shot came from. Most of these people have seen it. Now they're waiting for a glimpse of Lee Harvey Oswald."

The crowds would be disappointed. Chief Curry canceled the original plan to move Oswald at four o'clock on Saturday afternoon after Will Fritz requested more time with Oswald. The captain mistakenly believed he was making progress.

Next morning, Curry reviewed his options with Captain Fritz as well as Deputy Chief M. W. Stevenson and Assistant Chief Charles Batchelor. One idea they considered was to move Oswald in an armored truck. Unfortunately the turreted models of the day couldn't fit down the vehicle ramp into the basement.

Curry then called Sheriff Decker, whose department generally handled prisoner transfers from City Hall to the county jail. "I told him we were finished interrogating Oswald, that we weren't making any real strides," Curry recalled to me. "We chatted a bit about a couple of threats we had received by phone."

Decker, famous for his role in the pursuit of outlaws Bonnie and Clyde as well as for running gambler Benny Binion out of town in the late 1940s, masked a sharp mind behind a slow Texas twang. He had taken a late-night call from an individual who promised "one hundred citizens, pure Americans" would grab Oswald and "kill that communist son of a bitch." Given that kind of sentiment in the community, Decker later told me, he saw nothing but downside in moving Oswald at a pre-announced daylight hour. As a consequence, the sheriff seemed content to leave Chief Curry in charge of the matter.

"When I told him his boys could pick up the prisoner at any time," Curry said, "he just sorta changed the subject. He wasn't in any real hurry. Looking back, I think he country-boyed me."

Jesse Curry bit the bullet. "So I told him I thought we had more manpower, and we'd bring him soon. I'd call him when we left the building." Curry hung up and turned to Stevenson and Batchelor.

"It's our deal," he said. "Let's get it done."

CHAPTER EIGHT

"Brother, You Won't Find Anything There"

After I saw Jack Ruby in the *News* cafeteria on Friday morning, he headed for our second-floor ad department to meet with Don Campbell, an ad salesman and another of my close friends. I had been married in Don's East Dallas house the year before.

Ruby complained to Campbell that the two venues he operated, the Carousel Club, his strip joint on Commerce, and the Vegas Club, an after-hours destination in the city's Oak Lawn district, weren't doing well financially. He also bragged a bit about his prowess at breaking up fights and riding herd on the numerous drunken yahoos who frequented his establishments. He told Campbell that he recently had a major altercation, in which he had to kick out two or three customers. "He said, 'They didn't know what hit them when I inserted myself,'" Don recalled. "He said it was a good thing he was in such good shape because 'you just can't find too many take-charge guys around.'"

Ruby was known to bully and abuse his patrons, especially if they were too tanked to fight back. In the spring of 1962 at the Carousel

Club, I saw him toss a drunk down a long flight of stairs to the street. Then Ruby ran after the man and kicked him as he scrambled out the front door. I couldn't figure out why he attacked this particular customer. The club was quiet. Things seemed to be going smoothly. As far as I could tell, the guy hadn't caused any trouble. Jack Ruby was mercurial, unstable. In seconds he could change from easy-going to fists-in-your-face furious for no apparent reason.

Campbell, the first witness to be called at Ruby's murder trial, testified that the club owner behaved on Friday as he normally did. He made no mention to Don of the president's visit. Campbell departed the office at 12:20, leaving Ruby to work out his customary tiny notice for the weekend papers, usually no more than three or four inches deep. John Newnam, another *News* ad salesman, walked into the department about this time and noticed Ruby seated near Campbell's desk, reading the morning paper. "Look at this dirty ad!" Ruby exclaimed in disgust as he pointed to Weissman and Schmidt's black-bordered announcement.

Newnam later recalled Ruby saying something to the effect that he couldn't imagine a Jew promulgating such a message of hatred. "We've seen too much of that already," he said.

At that moment, someone ran into the room shouting, "The president's been shot! The president's been shot! I just heard it on the radio!"

Everyone gathered to watch the news on the television in promotion director Dick Jeffrey's office. The set was tuned of course to WFAA, where anchor Jay Watson had just interrupted *The Julie Benell Show*, a local women's program, to break the news.

"You'll excuse the fact that I am out of breath," said Watson, clearly fuddled, doing an impromptu standup from some anonymous corner of the station's newsroom. "But about ten or fifteen minutes ago a tragic thing—from all indications at this point—has happened to the city of Dallas."

Ad man Dick Saunders watched Ruby with the others as Watson read United Press International's newsbreak on the assassination:

"President Kennedy and Governor Connally have been cut down by assassin's bullets in Dallas."

"He sat there staring, unbelieving, at the television set," said Saunders of Ruby. "He was virtually speechless, quite unusual for Jack Ruby."

Ruby watched the unfolding tragedy for about thirty minutes; then he grabbed a telephone. His first call was to Andrew Armstrong, one of his employees at the Carousel Club. "We're going to close the club," several ad salesmen overheard Ruby tell Armstrong. "I don't know what else to do." Next, Ruby called his sister, Eva Grant, who also had an excitable nature. She seemed as devastated by the news as her brother. "My God! What do they want?!" she screamed into the receiver.

As Ruby put down the phone, he said to Newnam, "John, I will have to leave Dallas."

Members of the Warren Commission would ask Ruby what he meant by the remark. "I don't know I said that," he told them. "But it is a funny reaction you feel. The city is terribly let down by the tragedy that happened. And I said, 'John, I am not opening up tonight.' And I don't know what else transpired. I know people were just heartbroken. . . . I left the building and went down, and I got in my car and I couldn't stop crying."

There's no doubt that Jack Ruby was highly agitated in the wake of the assassination. For the next two days, he was a blur around Dallas. He left the *News,* arrived at the Carousel Club about a quarter to two on Friday, and set to work with Andrew Armstrong, notifying employees by telephone that the bar would be closed that night.

A couple of hours later, Ruby decided to close the Carousel for three days. He instructed Larry Crafard, a clean-up guy, handyman, and part-time bartender who lived at the club, to post a notice to that effect in the front window. "But don't put it out until dark," he ordered, "so they [his competitors] won't know in advance."

Ruby had a manic need to talk, if not listen, after the assassination. He called his friend, Ralph Paul, who owned the Bull Pen Drive-In, a hamburger joint in Arlington, midway between Dallas and Fort Worth, and advised Paul to close his business too. He tried repeatedly to reach Alice Nichols, a former girlfriend. He also called his youngest sister, Eileen Kaminsky, in Chicago. She later said her brother was "crying incessantly. He couldn't seem to stop. He told me he was going to leave Dallas, that he could never live this down."

As the hours passed, a crazed grandiosity crept into Ruby's remarks. He'd learned at the *News* that Bernard Weissman placed the offensive full-page ad and somehow connected that to the fact that he and Weissman both were Jews. The "dirty ad" deeply upset him, Ruby told many of the people he telephoned.

He called Temple Shearith Israel in Dallas to inquire about the schedule of evening services and then finally reached Alice Nichols to inform her that he'd be attending at eight o'clock. Ruby showed up for the final few minutes of the service. Afterward he spoke with Rabbi Hillel Silverman about his sister Eva's recent operation but made no mention of the murdered president.

Several people recalled another theme of his conversations in these hours was "those poor Kennedy kids" as well as John's and Caroline's widowed mother. Ruby later told reporters, including me, his motive for killing Lee Harvey Oswald was to spare Jacqueline Kennedy the pain of Oswald's trial, at which she'd likely be forced to testify.

After sharing a late delicatessen dinner with Eva at her apartment on Friday night, Ruby headed for City Hall. He was a familiar figure to many cops in Dallas, and so it was not surprising (though appalling) that Jack Ruby could insinuate himself into the continuing tumult on the third floor. Following Oswald's midnight remarks to the press, Ruby edged up to District Attorney Wade. "Hi, Henry," he said. Don't you know me? I'm Jack Ruby. I run the Vegas Club."

The next thing the DA knew, Ruby had reporter Ike Pappas from television station WNEW in New York in front of him, ready to conduct an exclusive interview. When Pappas was through, Ruby had a disc jockey from local radio station KLIF on the phone, also eager for an interview. "I thought he felt he was some kind of editor," Wade told me afterward. "It was hard to get rid of him."

Bob Jarboe, an Associated Press photographer sent to the station to get a photo of Wade, found that every time he had the DA centered in his lens, it seemed Jack Ruby would pop out of nowhere and put his chin on Wade's shoulder, ruining the shot. "I sure wish I would have gone ahead and taken the picture anyway," Jarboe later said.

It would have been a prize image.

From City Hall, Ruby traveled over to KLIF with a bag of sandwiches for the staff. Then, about four in the morning, he appeared at the *Times Herald*, where he spoke with Roy Pryor, an employee in the composing room who'd just completed his shift. Ruby told Pryor about attending Oswald's press conference. He called Oswald "a little weasel of a guy" and turned tearful and agitated when he talked of the now fatherless Kennedy children.

A half hour later, Ruby went home to his inexpensive, one-bedroom apartment in Oak Cliff to awaken George Senator, a friend who had been sleeping on his couch for the past few weeks. He also called Larry Crafard at the club, excitedly instructing Crafard to meet him and Senator at the Nichols Garage adjacent to the club and to bring a Polaroid camera.

Ruby had just seen a billboard urging the impeachment of U.S. Supreme Court Chief Justice Earl Warren and intended to take pictures of it. Senator later testified at Ruby's trial that his friend was upset both about the billboard's message and the Weissman ad in the *News*. "He said he couldn't understand anything of this nature being in the newspaper," said Senator in court. "He said it was a crime for something like this to appear in the paper. He said he thought the John Birch Society or the Communist Party or a combination of both was behind the billboard and the ad."

Senator would later capitalize on his association with the soon-to-be-notorious club owner by selling off Ruby's wardrobe and then some. Jack Ruby owned just two suits, for which he could not have paid more than fifty dollars apiece. Yet his ex-house guest sold at least four "authentic" Jack Ruby suits for as much as $300 each.

Recalling that the *News* ad had included a post office box address for Weissman's and Schmidt's American Fact-Finding Committee, Ruby, after a long night of dashing around Dallas, went to the downtown post office, where an employee refused to provide the box holder's name.

Ruby couldn't sleep, so he watched television at home through the morning. By about one that afternoon, he was seen in Dealey Plaza, walking around, talking to people, and handling the wreaths that mourners had placed around the scene of the assassination. It is possible that Ruby had come to Dealey Plaza because, like Dan Rather and so many other people, he expected Oswald to be transferred to the county jail that afternoon.

Wes Wise, a KRLD sportscaster and later mayor of Dallas, saw Ruby in the plaza that day and later described him to the Warren Commission as extremely wrought up. A policeman who pointed out Oswald's sixth-floor perch for Ruby remembered him as morose, obviously troubled.

He was growing ever more frenzied as well. Saturday afternoon Ruby was spotted at Sol's Turf Bar on Commerce, a favorite old haunt, as well as at the closed Carousel Club and up Commerce Street at police headquarters at City Hall. Frank Bellochio, a jewelry store owner Ruby encountered that day at Sol's, said that Ruby ranted on about the ad, darkly insisting that it was part of a plot against Jews in Dallas. As he showed his three Polaroids of the Impeach Earl Warren billboard around the bar, a patron asked if he could have one of them. Ruby said no. According to this witness's later testimony, he "acted like it was a big scoop or something."

Ruby was still working the phones hard that afternoon. In one call from the Nichols Garage to Ken Dowe, a KLIF announcer, Ruby discussed Oswald's coming transfer to the county jail. "You know I'll be there," he told Dowe.

About four o'clock on Saturday afternoon, Ruby called his lawyer, Stanley Kaufman. "He told me he had tried to get Weissman's address at the post office," Kaufman explained to me a few days later, "and said he was 'helping law enforcement.' He was rabid about the Weissman ad. He thought the black border had an inner meaning, proof that the man knew the president was going to be assassinated. I've seen him worked up lots of times, but on this afternoon he was really frantic."

Ruby appears to have spent most of the time between four and eight o'clock that day at his sister Eva Grant's apartment, calling people, complaining to them about Weissman. When he and his sister couldn't find Weissman in the phone book, they concluded the name was an alias. In the midst of it all, Ruby also telephoned Russ Knight, a KLIF on-air personality known as The Weird Beard, and talked to Knight about the billboard. According to Knight, Ruby asked him during this call, "Who *is* Earl Warren, anyway?"

Ruby took a one-hour nap at his sister's apartment on Saturday evening—his first real rest since Thursday—and was back at his own apartment at half past nine to take a call from nineteen-year-old Karen Bennett Carlin, one of his strippers. Carlin, who performed as Little Lynn, needed money, a simple business problem for Jack Ruby that nonetheless would later bear critically on the issue of his frame of mind and intent the following morning. According to George Senator, Ruby and Carlin exchanged angry words over the telephone, followed by Ruby's promise that he'd meet her at the Carousel Club in an hour.

Still another incidental character, Lawrence Meyers, a friend from Ruby's Chicago days, was in town on business, staying in a local hotel. Ruby called Meyers, who later reported that his old friend was "incensed" that other strip-club owners were staying open over the weekend, which meant lost revenue. Ruby raged to Meyers about the ad, the billboard, and the harm they might do to local Jews. "I've got to do something about this," he said to Meyers, who was unsure if his friend meant to "do something" about his competitors or Lee Harvey Oswald. He and Ruby agreed to meet for dinner on Sunday night.

In the meantime, Karen Carlin and her husband were waiting in front of the Carousel Club, impatient for their money. When Ruby didn't show, Karen called him from the Nichols Garage next door, pleading for at least enough money for the two to get home to Fort Worth. At Ruby's request, garage worker Huey Reeves gave Carlin five dollars, made out a receipt for her to sign, and time-stamped it at 10:33 p.m. Half an hour later, Ruby appeared at the garage, repaid Reeves his five dollars and then, agitated as ever, went upstairs to make some calls from the Carousel Club phone.

Among those he reached was Breck Wall, who operated a popular revue called *Bottoms Up*, then playing across Commerce at the Adolphus. Since the show had been cancelled that night because of the assassination, Wall was visiting relatives down in Galveston, where he took Ruby's call.

They discussed Oswald and the killings, Wall later remembered, but Ruby seemed more interested in discussing Dallas promoters Abe and Barney Weinstein, owners of Abe's Colony Club and the Theater Lounge, which featured weekly amateur strip shows that, according to Ruby, were killing the Carousel Club's business. Ruby was doing everything he could to close down the Weinsteins' operation, and he solicited Wall's views on whether the performers' union, the American Guild of Variety Artists (AGVA), would support or oppose him.

Jack Ruby was a very public presence in Dallas from Friday the twenty-second to Sunday the twenty-fourth, reaching out to—pestering—dozens of acquaintances in person and by telephone. However, contrary to a common assertion, there is absolutely no evidence that any of these people were his alleged underworld cronies. Ruby made one of his final calls of the night at a quarter to one to check on his sister Eva. Then he went home and was asleep by half past one, he later told police.

Lee Harvey Oswald's brother, Robert, was five years older than Lee. He worked in the marketing department at Acme Brick in Denton, the same small town where Larry Grove and I finally tracked down Chief Whaley, asleep in his cab. On Friday the twenty-second, Robert and some business associates had just finished their regularly scheduled luncheon meeting and were departing the restaurant when the cashier informed them that the president had been shot.

Back in his office, Robert turned on his radio to hear someone named Harvey Lee Oswald described as JFK's accused killer. The announcer soon added that a Dallas policeman had been shot dead as well. Then he repeated the suspect's name, getting it right this time: Lee Harvey Oswald. "That's my kid brother," Robert mumbled in amazement to no one in particular. "Something must have shown on my face," he later told me, "because the receptionist at the company began to cry."

That afternoon, as Robert grappled with the enormity of his kid brother's alleged crimes, the Dallas police began the first of their several interrogation sessions with Lee. The cops also brought Marina in for questioning. Her new baby, Rachel, and Ruth Paine accompanied her into the interview room that afternoon.

Following her session with the police, Marina, Rachel, and Mrs. Paine returned to the Paine residence in Irving, where they soon received a visit from the writer Tommy Thompson, then working for *Life* magazine, and his photographer, Allan Grant. The journalists had driven out to the Paine house with no expectation of encountering Marina or the girls or Marguerite Oswald, who was also on hand. But they were quick to seize the opportunity. Grant immediately began taking pictures. Marguerite just as quickly told him to stop.

"We should be paid for that!" she shouted, and suggested that $2,000 to $2,500 would be appropriate.

As Thompson tried to get his managing editor, George Hunt, on the phone in New York to approve a payment, Oswald's mother asked if the *Life* team could give them a ride over to Dallas so they could visit Lee at the jail. Thompson immediately said, "Sure," and then suggested that *Life* put them up at the Adolphus so they could be close to the jail. Marina, just returned from Dallas police headquarters, demurred, however. She did not want to wake her sleeping daughters. So it was agreed that the group would drive over on Saturday morning.

Thompson and Grant sat in their car outside the Paine house that Friday night, waiting for all the lights to go out, before returning to Dallas for a couple of hours of sleep. Next morning, the journalists sneaked the Oswalds into the Adolphus. Robert Oswald was on hand as well. Thompson was stymied by Marina's poor English and lost precious time coming up with a translator, a Russian-speaking pediatrician.

Then FBI agents came to the room, looking to conduct their own interrogation. Both Robert and Marguerite refused to let Marina go with the feds, however, "Until we can talk to Lee."

A deal was struck.

About noon on Saturday, the twenty-third, Robert arrived at the Dallas police department to visit Lee. Jim Bowie, one of Henry Wade's top assistants, met with him beforehand and laid out for Robert the already persuasive case that his younger brother had killed Kennedy and Tippit. Bowie raised the possibility that Lee might tell Robert exactly what his role had been in the killings, clearly hoping Robert would encourage Lee to do so and report what he learned. Robert, who was not particularly close to his younger brother and saw him only occasionally, nevertheless felt a basic familial bond. He promised Bowie nothing.

Robert Oswald's last moments with his younger brother were spent in a small visiting room on the fifth floor of City Hall. A Plexiglas partition separated the two.

Lee spoke first via the telephone.

"How are you?"

"Fine," Robert answered.

He noted cuts and bruises on Lee's face, but his brother assured him that the police were treating him all right.

"I cannot or would not say anything because the line apparently is tapped," Lee advised, then proceeded to monopolize the next two or three minutes, speaking in a strange, mechanical voice, saying, as Robert recalled to the Warren Commission, very little worth remembering.

"I was not talking to the Lee I knew," Robert later wrote in his diary.

He steered the conversation toward family matters, learning from Lee that he had a new niece, one-month-old Rachel. Lee said he'd wanted a boy, "but you know how that goes."

Eventually, Robert took up the big question.

"Lee, what the Sam Hill is going on?"

"What are you talking about?"

"They've got you charged with shooting a police officer and murdering the president. They've got your rifle and pistol."

"Do not," Lee cautioned, "form any opinion on the so-called evidence."

His tone was inappropriately flippant, which bothered Robert deeply. He later told me that he stared hard into Lee's eyes. "I was pretty intense. I was looking for some kind of reaction from him, anything at all. But there was absolutely no expression. He knew why I was looking so intensely at him. He said, 'Brother, you won't find anything there.' And he was right. There was nothing."

Later that afternoon, as Robert recounted the visit to his wife, Vada, and her parents, he broke into tears. "I didn't know exactly what to believe yet," he told me. "I thought there'd be time to talk more to him, to find out. But it wasn't to be."

Lee glowered later that afternoon as the police escorted Marina into the room, followed by Marguerite. "Why did you bring that fool with you?" he snapped in Russian. "I don't want to talk to her."

"She's your mother," Marina scolded him, also in Russian. "Of course she came."

Marguerite couldn't understand a word of the conversation and later said she suspected her son and daughter-in-law were keeping information from her.

Perhaps mindful of how prisoners were routinely treated in her country, Marina's first concern was Lee's physical well-being. "Have they been beating you?" she asked.

"Don't worry about me," he answered and then quickly changed the subject, asking after his daughters. Marina told me she feared saying anything that might get her husband into even deeper trouble.

"I asked him if we could talk about things," she explained, "important things. Are they listening in?"

"Of course we can't talk about anything important," he answered.

Unaware that the Mannlicher-Carcano was already in police custody, she asked him, "What about the gun?"

"It's a mistake," he answered with a smile. "I'm not guilty."

Marina was also unaware that Detectives Moore, Rose, and Stovall had recovered copies of the photo she'd taken of Lee with his guns from Ruth Paine's garage that afternoon. She had rounded up two other copies of the picture, which she placed in her shoe that day and destroyed that night.

Lee again mentioned the New York attorney John Abt to Marina and said he still hoped to reach Abt. "He said, 'There are people who will help me. We are not alone,'" she recalled. Marina began to cry. She later told me that she knew almost from his first words that Lee was guilty. The shock of that realization was compounded by worries that she and her two girls now had no money, no provider, and no permanent place to live. Moreover, all three bore a universally infamous surname. Would someone try to hurt them? In the end, would U.S. authorities ship her and her daughters back to the Soviet Union?

Consumed by these fears, yet loyal in her way to her husband, Marina was deeply conflicted as the guards came to escort Lee away from the Plexiglas partition. She told him for the last time ever that she loved him, and then he was gone.

·· ╫╪╫ ··

Jesse Curry, who resigned as Dallas police chief in March 1966 and died of a heart attack fourteen years later, was haunted to his grave by the events of Sunday morning, November 24, 1963.

The criticism that Curry and his department took for failing adequately to protect President Kennedy on Friday the twenty-second was in part mitigated by the speed with which the Dallas police apprehended Lee Harvey Oswald and brought him in alive. But then came the Sunday disaster. For years afterward, Curry received regular hate mail accusing him of everything from incompetency to complicity in Oswald's murder, often linking him to the Kennedy and Tippit killings too.

Curry never shirked his responsibility for handling the transfer as he did and never tried to weasel out of the decision even as he freely conceded it was a bad choice. Had he the chance to do it again, the chief told me, "I would have cleared all of the newsmen out of the building. I know that would have been very unpopular, but in view of what happened, it would have been the thing to do."

Curry always denied that he was put under any official pressure to display his prisoner to the press—as in the now familiar "perp walk," a staple of modern television news—even though it was widely rumored that Dallas City Manager Elgin Crull instructed the chief to make Oswald's transfer a public event in order to show that the accused killer had not been abused by the police. This was no trivial point at the time. Earl Rose, the Dallas County medical examiner, later revealed that unnamed members of the Oswald family insisted upon personally examining his body for signs of injury before he was autopsied.

Late on Saturday, over the vehement objections of his senior staff, Chief Curry told reporters they wouldn't miss anything next morning if they were on hand at City Hall by ten. Captain Fritz was among those who didn't like the idea of a public transfer. He suggested using an armored car as a decoy.

Detective Jim Leavelle, forever famous in the Beers and Jackson photographs as the cop in the light suit and Stetson who was handcuffed to Oswald, told me he advised Curry to "double-cross" the media and move the suspect by surprise—a strategy that I personally expected Curry would carry out. I thought it made no sense to move Oswald in public.

But the chief was adamant.

"I told them—promised them—they'd see the man moved," Curry replied to Leavelle. "I want them to see we haven't abused him. And the only way to do that is to see the transfer."

There's no doubt that Jack Ruby, along with the rest of world, knew of Chief Curry's plan to move Oswald on Sunday morning. It was announced on radio and television numerous times. If, as some conspiracy buffs have surmised, Ruby was part of a plan to silence Oswald, it stands to reason that the club owner would have appeared with his gun at City Hall by the appointed hour, ten o'clock. Instead, Ruby was awakened that morning by a call from his cleaning lady, Elnora Pitts. He appears to have been in no hurry to rise, as was his custom, and he consumed a leisurely breakfast.

George Senator told me that Ruby headed to the apartment building laundry room with a load of wash at about nine o'clock. Telephone company records show that at exactly 10:19 a.m., a still-irate Karen Carlin called Ruby at home from Fort Worth. She demanded the twenty-five dollars that she needed for rent and groceries. Ruby told her he'd wire the money by Western Union later that morning.

I awoke about half past nine, turned on the television, and was surprised to learn that Oswald was still at the police lockup, still awaiting transfer that morning to Sheriff Decker's custody. Oh, my God, I thought. Curry's taking a big risk. "Look," I said to my wife, "we've got to get down there!" I didn't shave. I didn't eat. We just threw on some clothes, and I drove like mad to City Hall.

Jack Ruby, meanwhile, had wired Karen Carlin her money from the nearest Western Union office and was walking back to his car, parked on Main Street, when he noticed a commotion a block away at City Hall. Curious, Ruby joined the crowd of onlookers. There was a lot of confusion, pushing and elbowing, especially now that the huge out-of-town and international press contingent had arrived, another consequence of Chief Curry's decision to make the move in public.

Security was fairly tight. My wife was refused access to the City Hall basement where the transfer was to be made. So she headed off to a downtown breakfast place, where I planned to join her in a few minutes. Police guards checked my credentials three times before allowing me into the area where Oswald was to be brought out of the elevator and escorted to the back seat of a waiting police cruiser.

I didn't see Ruby in the basement even though he was standing perhaps fifteen feet from me as Detectives Leavelle and L. C. Graves brought their handcuffed prisoner toward the car. I remember a lot of talking and jostling and reporters trying to peer around and over other reporters hoping for a glimpse of Oswald.

Then, in the midst of it all, came that *pop* sound again. It was 11:21 a.m. Detective Thomas McMillon later testified that Ruby snarled, "You rat son of a bitch!" at Oswald as he shot him. But all I heard was that *pop!* Just once this time, muffled and faint. Jack Ruby's Colt Cobra .38 sounded like a toy.

CHAPTER NINE

"My Son Was a Hero"

T he first person ever to be murdered on national television expired in Trauma Room No. 2 at Parkland Hospital at 1:07 p.m. that Sunday, directly across the hall from where President Kennedy died of his gunshot wounds forty-eight hours earlier. Oswald might have died on the same table as JFK had not hospital administrator Jack Price diverted his gurney from Trauma Room No. 1 at the last moment.

Next day, shortly after the nation watched the president's somber, dignified funeral on television, Oswald was buried in a gray casket on a barren hillside at Rose Hill Cemetery in Fort Worth. Two preachers who agreed to officiate failed to show, so the service was led by the Reverend Louis Saunders, a Disciple of Christ minister and executive secretary of the Fort Worth Council of Churches.

Marguerite Oswald and Robert, who had made the funeral arrangements, were at the graveside as were Marina and the girls. Six reporters served as pall bearers, including Mike Cochran, the Associated Press correspondent. Cochran refused to participate initially. Then the competition, Preston McGraw of United Press International, stepped up and accepted the job. "At that point, I didn't have a choice," Cochran remembers. Besides Cochran and McGraw, the other newsmen serving as pallbearers were Jerry Flemmons, Bunky McConal, and Ed Horn from the *Fort Worth Star-Telegram*, and a sixth reporter from a Midwest newspaper.

Perhaps two dozen more reporters and photographers stood forty more or less respectful feet away as Reverend Saunders conducted Oswald's brief rites. "We are not here to stand in judgment of him," the minister said to the press afterward. "We are here only to lay him to rest."

Reporters behaved in an uncommonly civil manner that day, says Cochran. "The media did not harass the family, not even the TV guys. Nobody intruded. It was respectful."

Later, when Jim Marrs, a well-known conspiracy buff, sold a photo to the AP, claiming it was a shot of Oswald in his casket, Cochran did his best to screw up the deal for Marrs. "I guess it was Oswald," he remembers. "I don't know. I just said to the AP, 'It doesn't look like him at all.'"

Given Lee Harvey Oswald's sorry life and ignoble death, the humble interment was no surprise. It was easy to see him circling the drain almost from the start. Born October 18, 1939, in New Orleans, Oswald never knew his father, Robert Edward Lee Oswald, second husband to the former Marguerite Claverie. An insurance premium collector, Oswald died of coronary thrombosis two months before Lee's birth.

According to several sources, the boy slept with Marguerite until he was eight years old—except for a few months when he was four or five and she placed him in the Bethlehem Orphanage Asylum with his brother Robert and their older half-brother, John Pic, from Marguerite's first marriage.

In 1945, Marguerite married a Boston industrial engineer, Edwin A. Ekdahl, and moved with Ekdahl to Dallas, where Lee began public school. John and Robert were sent off to military school in Mississippi. Ekdahl divorced Marguerite in 1948, claiming in court documents that she endlessly nagged about money and physically abused him.

John and Robert joined the armed services at their first chance as would Lee. By the age of ten, he'd attended six different public schools and was becoming a behavioral problem.

In the summer of 1952, Marguerite suddenly decided that she and Lee would move to New York City to live with John Pic and his young wife, Margaret, who themselves were guests in a Bronx apartment that Margaret's mother rented. Marguerite and Lee arrived unannounced and stayed with the Pics until John, annoyed that his mother refused to get a job or discipline his young half-brother, ordered them to leave.

John Pic told the Warren Commission that his mother didn't think Margaret was good enough for him and told him so repeatedly. "Naturally, I resented this," he testified, "because I put my wife before my mother any day." The flashpoint came one afternoon when Lee and Marguerite erupted into an argument over what channel to watch on the Pics' television. To Margaret Pic's horror, the twelve-year-old hit his mother and menaced her with a pocketknife.

When Margaret told her husband of the incident that night, John Pic confronted his mother and half-brother. Marguerite downplayed the episode. Lee, according to John's testimony, "became real hostile toward me. When this happened, it perturbed my wife so much that she told him they were going to leave whether they liked it or not."

The half-brothers never spoke to one another again.

Marguerite and Lee moved into a tiny apartment in the Bronx. He seldom attended school, preferring instead to watch television, ride the subway around town, and visit the zoo. Finally truancy officials nabbed him and sent the thirteen-year-old to a youth facility for a six-week evaluation.

Psychiatrists there saw an intelligent nonconformist with a questionable role model, receiving unreliable adult supervision. One of them, Dr. Renatus Hartogs, noted, "Lee is a youngster with superior mental endowments, functioning presently in the bright-normal range of mental efficiency. His abstract thinking and his vocabulary are well developed. No retardation in school subjects could be found despite truancy. Oswald's IQ was measured at an above-average 118.

Evelyn Strickman, a social worker, wrote, "There is a pleasant, appealing quality about this emotionally starved, affectionless youngster, which grows as one speaks to him." Lee told her his favorite television show was *I Led Three Lives*, a popular series based on the adventures of FBI double agent, Herbert Philbrick. He also said he wanted more than anything to join the U.S. Marines, just like his big brother Robert.

He watched *I Led Three Lives* compulsively, Robert told the PBS program *Frontline* in 1993. "I think he just liked the atmosphere that you could do anything you wanted to do, that anything you could imagine you could do. To me, it gets down to what happened later on. That was a training ground for his imagination."

When her youngest son was released from the youth facility, Marguerite moved with him to New Orleans, where his attitude did not improve. At sixteen, Lee forged her name to a note informing his school that he no longer would be attending classes, inasmuch as the family was moving out of the district. Then he forged a second document attesting that he was seventeen and thus eligible to join the military.

Marguerite signed the paper for him, but the Marines refused him, telling Oswald to try again in a year. Finally, in 1956, his mother signed a proper permission waiver in Dallas, and at last, Lee was allowed to enlist.

This was a young man who most definitely wanted to get away from mom. And who could blame him?

Oswald hated the discipline and the rigors of barracks life. His fellow Marines called him "Ozzie Rabbit" for the way his ears stuck out, and they derided him for reading a Russian-language newspaper. The other guys also made merciless fun of him when he accidentally shot himself in the arm.

He retreated into radical left-wing ideology and decided, while still in the service, that what he really wanted to do was visit the Soviet Union. With his mother's help—and the Marines' eager approval—he secured an early discharge.

Marguerite, who'd recently been injured in a fall, expected her boy to come stay with her in Fort Worth. But after two days, Lee announced he was headed for New Orleans to find work on a ship. His mother was furious. "After all," she told me later, "I got him out so he could come and help me out financially."

A short while later, Lee put even more distance between himself and his mother. He defected to the Soviet Union.

⸻

Few people have ever so deeply annoyed me as did Marguerite Oswald. And of all the things I disliked about her, none irritated me more than her voice. It was strange—unique in my experience—a jarring combination of birdlike singsong, childish whine, and predatory threat that invaded your head like a dental drill. She would not stop talking.

I first heard from Mrs. Oswald in early December 1963, when she called me at the *News* to complain about the escape route story I'd written with Larry Grove. "Obviously" Larry and I had gotten our information from a government leak, and she wanted to correct some mistakes.

Next—and this was typical of Marguerite Oswald—she suggested we call the *Star-Telegram* to arrange a car and driver for her to come visit us at the *News* in Dallas. It was a trick I would have loved to play on my friends in Fort Worth, but I told her instead that Larry and I would drive over to meet with her.

No photo ever really captured Marguerite Oswald. In pictures, she usually appeared behind a pair of dark-rimmed glasses, jaw set, moist eyes about to flood with tears, the very image of a doughty American mom fighting to clear her infamous son's name. In truth, she was supremely egotistical, combative, devious, and smart.

I knew before I met her that she was already selling interviews and artifacts to the highest bidder. In fact, she tried to open negotiations for a paid interview with *Life* magazine within twenty-four hours of President Kennedy's death. My single interest in her at the time was to learn if I could determine how Lee and Marina could afford their trip to Texas from the Soviet Union in the spring of 1962. I knew Oswald had little or no money and assumed the trip had been costly.

When Larry and I arrived at her tiny, cluttered house in Fort Worth, a pair of Japanese reporters waiting for a cab were sitting in her living room. They smiled a lot but seemed confused as Marguerite plunked news clips into their laps and proceeded to tell them who in the articles was a CIA agent or an FBI plant.

They greeted their cab's arrival with looks of genuine relief.

My first lesson in interviewing Marguerite Oswald was that you didn't because you couldn't. She didn't exchange thoughts and ideas but simply talked and talked and talked, oblivious to any distraction as she careened from subject to subject according to some interior logic that I never figured out.

The one subject Mrs. Oswald did not touch on in our first meeting was her youngest son's very recent murder. Instead she ranted at length about Marina and Ruth Paine. "Marina's mixed up in this," she said, "and that Paine woman. They conspired. I don't know the whole story, but I know enough."

She briefly turned her attention to our article, insisting we were wrong about her son taking a bus and then a cab. "And why would he go on past his rooming house?" she wanted to know. "And so he had a pistol! Half the young men in Dallas have a pistol!"

Then it was back to her daughter-in-law. "Do you know why I didn't get to see my son for more than a year?" she said. "Because of Marina. Marina wanted him away from me. Why, they didn't even tell me they were moving out of Fort Worth! I was with them the afternoon before they left, and they never told me!"

Larry and I exchanged a glance. I was beginning to feel some compassion for Lee Harvey Oswald.

"Now she won't even talk to me," Marguerite continued. "She's in protected [sic] custody somewhere, but they won't tell me where." Somehow this fact reminded Mrs. Oswald that she once gave Marina a pocket watch that belonged to Lee's dad. "I guess she thinks that's hers now too," she said with a huff.

Try as I might, I could not get her to focus on the single issue that interested me that day. After enduring her rambling tirade for an hour or so, I would have been content just to leave.

A short while later, she was back in my face again. I did a radio show in which, as I recall, I mentioned that Oswald had purchased both his rifle and handgun by mail and that I thought it interesting how he and Marina seemed to get back from Russia to the United States so easily.

Marguerite called to complain, first of all, about how she, not her dead son, was being treated by the press. Almost every day, she said, there was some sort of attack on her in the papers or on television. Then she turned to my radio remarks, calling them "scurrilous, totally absurd, and ill-informed."

She was just warming up.

"As far as how he and Marina got back," Marguerite informed me, "I was the one. I sent him the money. Now what do you have to say about that?"

I believe I apologized to her and then asked how much the trip had cost her. "Oh, $800 or $900," she answered. "I don't remember." Much later, I learned that she contributed nothing to her son's travel expenses. His brother Robert sent Lee several hundred dollars. The Red Cross and other agencies made up the rest.

"I guess you know my son was an agent for the federal government," she said, "and they just threw him away. I can prove that." That's where I stopped Marguerite and said I'd like to come over and see her proof. During this period, there were rumors everywhere that Oswald once worked for the FBI or the CIA as a paid informant. I was skeptical but willing to be convinced.

One reporter who felt certain Oswald had worked for the government was Alonzo "Lonnie" Hudkins of the *Houston Post*. Lonnie called me constantly, hoping I'd uncovered something to move the story along. In time, I grew tired of Lonnie's queries, especially since I doubted his sources were that good. One day as I was busily juggling deadline stories for *Newsweek*, where I was then a stringer, and the *Times of London* as well as a weekend piece for the *News*, Lonnie called once more and asked me, "You hear anything about this FBI link with Oswald?" Tired of him bugging me, I said to him, "You got his payroll number, don't you?"

"Yeah, yeah," Lonnie said.

I reached over on my desk for a telegram and read part of a Telex number to him.

"Yeah, yeah," he said, "that's it. That's the same one I've got." I knew that if Lonnie accepted the number as legitimate, he had nothing. He said he'd check his sources and get back to me.

Weeks passed, and I forgot about the call until January 1, 1964, when Hudkins published a front page article in the *Post*, alleging that Oswald may have been a federal operative. Naturally the story caused quite a stir. Members of the newly created Warren Commission summoned several top Texas law enforcement officials and advisers to Washington to discuss the development, including Waggoner Carr, the state Attorney General, Dallas DA Henry Wade, and his assistant Bill Alexander; J. Edgar Hoover of course told the commission that the story was not true. The Texas folks denied any knowledge of where Hudkins got his story, and the story pretty much died—for a while.

Lonnie never disclosed his source for the bogus number, and I didn't admit to it for at least several years.

FBI Agent Joe Hosty was among those upset over the Hudkins story. In *Assignment Oswald*, he castigated me not only for the Jack Revill story that Jim Ewell and I published but also for being, along with Bill Alexander, the supposed source of Hudkins's fantasy.

When Hosty later called me, it was in part to apologize for that mistake. "Just wanted you to know that I visited with Hudkins later," he said, "and understand that it was *his* contention, not yours and Alexander's, about the alleged financial connection between the bureau and Oswald. I always admit my errors."

Then Hosty went off on a curious tangent.

"If you want to really get to the truth about what happened," he said, "dig into Oswald's days in Mexico. They tried to keep most of that from me, but I found out the connections and why." According to Hosty, Cuban sources had told the bureau that on Oswald's trip to Mexico City just weeks before the assassination, he had boasted of his intention to kill President Kennedy. The former FBI man said he believed that one or more people in Mexico put Oswald up to following through. "This man was easily led," said Hosty, "and somebody obviously . . . led him."

Federal investigative files that remain classified might someday substantiate or disprove Hosty's contentions.

Marguerite Oswald also didn't have any credible evidence her son worked as an informant for the government. On this visit, she told me that she was writing a book about her son, a project that she'd originally embarked on over Lee's strong objections when he first returned from the Soviet Union.

This time, before I was able to make my escape, she tried to sell me pictures of Lee, his letters from Russia, a couple of school report cards. When I tried to steer her back toward a substantive conversation, she snapped, "I guess you came here expecting me to tell you all I know without any payment. Well, those days are gone forever."

From then on, Marguerite was generally upset at something in the *News* all the time, but she also freely berated me for pieces that turned up elsewhere such as the *New York Times* or *Detroit Free Press*.

I was hardly her only victim. She was a tireless adversary. One of her targets was Howard Brennan, the only eyewitness to the assassination. Brennan said he watched Marguerite on *The Johnny Carson Show*, where she attacked him (Brennan), not by name, but he felt everybody knew whom she was talking about.

"She impugned my integrity," he wrote in his memoir, "and said, 'The witness is blind as a bat; he wears glasses.'" Actually Brennan did wear glasses after January 1964. His eyes were injured in an industrial sandblasting accident, which affected his eyesight. He wrote in the mid-1980s, "After that, my vision wasn't what it had been before the accident, yet even today I am not 'blind as a bat.' My vision is 20/20 with glasses. Before the accident, my eyes were exceptional."

Although he received an avalanche of phone calls in the weeks after the assassination, one caller who bugged the Brennans particularly was a woman who would never give her name. Her calls came every two or three weeks, he recollected. "Louise [Mrs. Brennan] said the woman's voice was familiar though she couldn't place it.

"The caller adamantly refused to give her name, but she did her best to discredit me. She would say, 'How can your husband have the audacity to be so sure he saw the man that killed Kennedy?' Louise tried not to argue with her though it was difficult because the caller questioned my eyesight as well as my integrity."

Eventually they just chalked the caller up as "another nut," as Brennan put it, and prepared to live with it. But one day the veil of anonymity finally slipped. As she launched once more into her telephone tirade, the woman snapped, "My son didn't do it." It was Marguerite Oswald.

I heard from Marguerite again after I'd reviewed one of the earliest conspiracy books, a ridiculous volume that argued Lee Harvey Oswald worked for both the CIA and the FBI and was part of a crack undercover hit team. Burning up the telephone lines from Fort Worth to Dallas, she threatened to ruin me "as a journalist for taking such liberties" and again promised to produce hard evidence that Lee was indeed an agent. "You'll see," she screeched. "I can't wait to see you eat this crow."

I never saw her again, but I was party to a particularly strange episode in which Marguerite played the starring role. On Mother's Day weekend, 1965, the writer Jean Stafford came to Dallas to do a major story on Mrs. Oswald for *McCall's* magazine. Jean was a wonderful writer—she went on to win the Pulitzer Prize for fiction in 1970—and had been married to a couple of other literary lions, the poet Robert Lowell and journalist A. J. Liebling.

Stafford ran into trouble at the outset. When her limo driver delivered her to Marguerite's door on Friday, a loud voice from inside shouted, "I can't let you in. They are going to have to pay me a lot more. I've done some research on *McCall's*, and I know what they are worth."

Stafford didn't know what to do. She was told the magazine would pay Marguerite $800. "I wasn't the type to deal with the money, to make bids and the like," she later told me. "And I was taken aback, not by the coarseness of the demand, but by the voice itself. You have to hear that woman angered to understand what I mean."

I told Jean that I understood fully. I knew from long experience how absolutely eerie it could get with her. "How much do you want?" Stafford yelled back through the front door.

"Thirteen hundred and fifty," Marguerite shrieked, "and they've got it!"

"Let me use the phone," Stafford replied. "I will call New York and see if they will agree to that."

Mrs. Oswald's truculence vanished at once. She opened the door and greeted Jean Stafford as she might an old friend. When the writer couldn't get anyone at *McCall's* to authorize the additional payment, she decided to guarantee the extra $550 herself. "I wasn't about to leave without something," Stafford said. She soon had reason to rue her determination.

Stafford spent several hours with Marguerite that day, mostly discussing Lee. Mrs. Oswald stunned the writer several times with her bold, revisionist views on the saga, most particularly her avowed belief that since her son was a government agent and that the assassination might have been an assignment, a mercy killing.

As Stafford later quoted Marguerite in her book, *A Mother in History*, "Now maybe Lee Harvey Oswald was the assassin. But does that make him a louse? No. No. Killing does not necessarily mean badness. You find killing in some very fine homes for one reason or another. And as we all know, President Kennedy was a dying man. So I say that it is possible that my son was chosen to shoot him in a mercy killing for the security of the country. And if this is true, it was a fine thing to do and my son is a hero."

Stafford wrote that she'd been "staggered by this cluster of fictions stated as irrefutable fact." Yet she somehow maintained her poise. "I had not heard that President Kennedy was dying."

"Oh yes," Marguerite said, explaining that Kennedy suffered from Atkinson's, a kidney disease.

Purposefully or otherwise, she'd confused it with Addison's disease, a nonfatal malfunction of the adrenal gland for which Kennedy was treated for several years.

Friday evening, Stafford dined with me and Lon Tinkle, the venerable book editor at the *News*. "It scared the devil out of me," she told us. "All in all she was polite, but there's something deadly about that woman. Maybe I won't go back tomorrow."

Lon and I argued that she should, but as a safety measure maybe keep the car and driver waiting outside.

That idea seemed to reassure her a bit. "I wish I could take pictures in that house," she said. "You won't believe what's she's got over her desk."

"The plaque?" I smiled. "The hero plaque?"

"God! You've seen it!" Stafford gasped in mock horror. Lon looked puzzled, so Jean explained, reaching into her purse for a small notepad so she could get the exact wording. "She's got this copper scroll, which says 'My son, Lee Harvey Oswald, even after his death has done more for his country than any other living human being. Signed Marguerite C. Oswald.'"

Saturday Stafford returned to Mrs. Oswald's house with two rented reel-to-reel tape machines. Marguerite had agreed to be recorded but only if she got an original copy of the tape too. I didn't envy Jean having to spend an entire, uninterrupted day with Marguerite and wasn't surprised to hear by telephone on Saturday evening that she was completely spent. "This is the toughest assignment I've ever had," she told me. "I don't feel like going back there tomorrow, but I left the tape recorders there, so I have to."

The third day, Mother's Day, Stafford stood at Marguerite's front door and again heard her loud voice coming from within. This time it was recorded. "She had decided to tape record a couple of hours for me on her own," Jean said later. "I guess I wasn't asking the right questions."

The big finale to the grueling, three-day marathon was to be a trip to Lee's grave. Marguerite climbed into the new Buick Skylark she'd bought with proceeds of the sale to *Esquire* magazine of Lee's letters to her from the Soviet Union. Jean sat next to her. The rented limo trailed behind.

As they entered the turnpike, Marguerite leaned toward Stafford and held out her hand for the fifteen-cent toll. Jean dug a dime and a nickel from her purse, but Marguerite did not withdraw her hand. Stafford looked at her questioningly. "Well," she said, "I have to return, Jean." So Stafford found a quarter and pressed it into Marguerite's palm.

"It seemed that everything she uttered got just a notch weirder," Stafford said over the telephone later that Sunday. "I found myself really afraid. She asked me if I would come back to Fort Worth and stay with her for the summer and write 'our' book together. When she asked me where I was staying tonight, I told her the SMU faculty club. I didn't know what she had in mind."

"Jean, SMU doesn't have a faculty club, at least not where guests stay," I said.

"I know. I know," she said. "I just told her that. I'm flying out early tonight." She then asked for an unusual favor. "Hugh, I am not going back to the hotel. I have most of my clothes with me. I'm going straight to Love Field. Would you hold these tapes for me and send them to me when you can?"

I agreed, not quite understanding why she didn't want to travel with the reels of tape. Apparently Jean had developed a Marguerite phobia, a deep dread not only of the woman but of anything she'd even touched, including the reels of tape, which she left for me at the Braniff counter. I picked them up the next morning and listened to them at home before forwarding them to Stafford in New York on Tuesday.

Six or seven years later, while I was working in Houston as the *Newsweek* bureau chief, I heard once more from Marguerite. She called me at home one Sunday about a story I'd just done on New Orleans District Attorney Jim Garrison and his sideshow investigation of the Kennedy assassination. I guess I was fairly curt with her, probably because she'd interrupted a football game I was watching on television.

In any event, she began shouting, as usual. "Your kids are gonna suffer!" she railed. "I can guarantee you that!" We hung up, and I thought about the conversation for a while. In my view, she was clearly disturbed and therefore probably capable of anything if the mood struck her. It thus seemed prudent that if Marguerite was threatening me, I should get it on tape.

About an hour later, I called her back, my tape machine recording the conversation. Her tone had changed completely. She was cordial. When I asked her bluntly if she'd meant the remark about my children as a threat, she said, "Oh, no. I will do more than that for you. I will make you eat the truth." Then, as if we were lifelong pals, she cooed, "I'm going to do a town hall appearance in Los Angeles next weekend. Why don't you come out and debate me? We both could make some money out of it."

It was the last time we talked. Marguerite died in 1981.

CHAPTER TEN

"Sometimes He Was a Little Bit Sick": Marina

Tommy Thompson never did get his interview with Marina that first weekend. Once other reporters discovered their gambit, Thompson and Grant spirited the Oswald women out of the downtown area and out to the Executive Inn near Love Field. Marguerite, of course, continued to insist on payment. Allan Grant later said he gave her two hundred dollars.

Robert Oswald, in the company of the FBI agents, planned to drive Marina, Marguerite, and the little girls to the safety of his in-laws' farm a few miles outside Fort Worth. But just after eleven on Sunday morning, as the agents' translator, Peter Gregory, and Robert arrived at the Executive Inn, word came via radio that Oswald had been attacked by a gunman in the City Hall basement. "Now don't get excited," one of them said to Robert, "but we've just got word that Lee's been shot."

Robert jumped back in his car and headed for Parkland Hospital, instructing the agents to take the Oswalds to the farm. Instead, they drove Marina and Marguerite around town without informing either woman that Lee was mortally wounded. Eventually, they did tell Marina that her husband had been shot but said he was not seriously hurt.

For reasons I've never ascertained, the unusual party eventually ended up at Chief Curry's house, of all places. Marina told me that the Currys were very welcoming, offering them drinks and making small talk. There, she said, Peter Gregory finally broke the news. "Get hold of yourself," Gregory said. "He's dead."

⚜

At the time of her husband's murder, Marina Oswald, then just twenty-two years old, had known Lee for less than three years—all but a few weeks of that time as his wife. Like Oswald, she never met her father, whom her mother cryptically indicated had disappeared soon after Marina's birth in 1941. Her mother died when Marina was sixteen.

Despite stern disapproval of relatives, the teenager began spending more and more time with a friendly prostitute named Irina. In his book, *Oswald's Tale*, Norman Mailer recounts the story of Irina's Afghan client who rapes Marina, then demands his money back after learning from Marina that she is a virgin. In Mailer's account, Marina complains of the assault, and Irina says, "What do you expect? Do you think you can go around forever and eat and do nothing for it?"

Marina was tiny. She was about five feet two, weighed less than a hundred pounds, and wore a size five dress. She was conventionally pretty, despite bad teeth. She drank heavily, chain smoked, and, according to Mailer, was rumored to have worked as a street hooker in her native Leningrad.

She met Lee Oswald on March 17, 1961, at a student party in Minsk, where he worked for twenty-three months in a radio factory and she studied to become a pharmacist. In his secret "Historic Diary," Oswald described the occasion: "Boring, but at the last hour

I am introduced to a girl with a French hairdo and red dress with white slippers. I dance with her and then ask to show her home."

Marina didn't lack for admirers at the party. Oswald counted five other guys also eager to escort her into the night. "Her name is Marina," he wrote. "We like each other right away. She gives me her phone number and departs home with a not-so-new friend in a taxi. I walk home."

The courtship revved up quickly and blossomed into marriage on the first of May, *the* red letter day in any communist land, as Lee Harvey Oswald most definitely was aware. Yet in the diary, Oswald dates his wedding day as April 31, which I doubt was a mistake. More likely it was a deliberate veiled reflection of his gathering disenchantment with Soviet life. He'd been plotting his return to the United States for months.

Nor was Marina the first girl Oswald proposed to that year. Ella Germain, whom he described as "a very attractive Russian Jew," worked with him at the Minsk radio plant. Ella caught his eye around the start of the year. "I think I'm in love with her," he wrote. "She has refused my more dishonorable advances." On January 2, he proposed to Ella and was rejected. "My love is real," he noted forlornly, "but she has none for me."

After wedding Marina, he admitted in the diary that his motive in marriage was to "hurt" Ella Germain but that he'd also grown to love Marina—who in any case was "madly in love with me from the very start."

According to Marina, this was typical self-flattery. "I felt sorry for him," Bob Fenley quoted her in the *Times Herald*, "because everybody hated him—even in Russia."

Whatever Marina's reason for marrying Lee or her hopes for their union, she was to be thoroughly disappointed. Oswald was a violent, petty tyrant who neither smoked nor drank and forbade his wife from doing so. He even banned lipstick.

Once they arrived in Texas, she was not allowed to speak any language except Russian in his presence even though Marina longed to practice English as part of her desire to secure U.S. citizenship. She and Lee fought frequently. Acquaintances reported that Marina often appeared covered with bruises left by her husband's fists.

After his murder, legions of generous strangers stepped forward to help Marina address her main concern: how to care for two small children with very little money and no safe, permanent shelter. At our first meeting, in March 1964, Marina told me that she feared presuming any further on Ruth Paine's charity. "The Secret Service people told me to stay away from her. They said the Paines had been put through enough already, and they said I had enough money to easily live. I didn't know. I wasn't sure."

The Feds were right about the money part. But they also made a second recommendation, that Marina seek help with the management of her money from an individual named James Herbert Martin. In light of Marina's experience, the agents' counsel of disengaging from Ruth Paine while engaging with Jim Martin had a disagreeable smell to it.

The first financial help Marina received was a check for $25,000 from a Philadelphia publisher. A river of money from all over the world followed. Some foreign news organizations compensated her in cash. Two whom I ushered into her presence told me they forked over $12,000 and $8,000 respectively for the pleasure of her company. There was no public accounting of the sums Marina received from donors, but I know it came to at least $200,000. She did even better once she got a firmer grasp of Western capitalism. In the end, her total haul greatly exceeded Marguerite's but was dwarfed by the mountain of money collected by Tippit's widow, Marie.

Published accounts pegged that amount at $750,000, which probably was a low estimate. Mrs. Tippit also benefited from the investment advice of several Dallas financial experts, who established a fortune in trusts for her at local banks.

The largely untold story of Marina's path from destitution to solvency was not without its share of intrigue, drama, fear, and pain. It began at a motel between Dallas and Fort Worth, the Inn at Six Flags in Arlington, where for a time the Secret Service kept her in protective custody. There Marina met Jim Martin, an assistant manager at the inn. Marina later claimed to the FBI that at first she believed Martin was simply in charge of cleaning her room.

Her relationship with him began six days after the assassination when Martin asked her to Thanksgiving dinner with his wife, Wanda, and their children at their home in suburban Garland. Before the end of the meal, the Martins had invited Marina to come live with them. She moved in a day or so later.

By the way, Marina's Dallas police protection squad followed her. Apparently she was unaware that one member of her security detail was Nick McDonald, the cop who helped capture Lee at the Texas Theater.

"He seemed nice," she said of Jim Martin to FBI agents Gobo Bogoslav and Wallace Heitman, "and I realized he knew more about money than I did." Martin went right to work. Since her English was quite shaky, he communicated with Marina via a Russian-speaking Secret Service agent, Leo Gopadze. Wheeling and dealing, her new business manager set up several paid press interviews, negotiated with movie companies, and explored other possible sources of income on her behalf. He also introduced her to lawyer John Thorne of Grand Prairie. Thorne soon became Marina's attorney.

Jim Martin had other designs on Marina Oswald as well. She later told the FBI that he pursued her romantically almost from the moment they met. He teased her, courted her, touched her, and begged her to love him. On New Year's Day, for example, he played a record by Mario Lanza and sang "some tunes of love" as Marina remembered, while Martin's eyes "ate me up."

Marina told Martin that she'd never marry him but she would be his lover if he liked. "Jim and I discussed plans," she told the bureau agents. "We planned that I would have my own house and he would come to visit me and we would be lovers." She claimed that particular part of their relationship was consummated just once, on Friday night, February 7, 1964, at the Willard Hotel in Washington, D.C., where she was to testify before the Warren Commission.

The biggest hurdle to the union was the Secret Service agents camped in the room next to hers. They made it difficult for Martin to sneak in and out. So Marina requested that the agents be removed. Within hours, Jim Martin and John Thorne took over the vacated room.

That night, she and Martin and little June Lee went to dinner, arriving back at the Willard about eight o'clock. When John Thorne finally fell asleep, Jim Martin slipped next door. "I took a bath," Marina told the FBI, "and was partly dressed when I reentered the bedroom. Jim finished undressing me, and thereafter we had sexual intercourse. It was with my consent, and I did not resist. Martin did not make me perform any unnatural sex acts."

Marina returned with Martin and Thorne to Dallas the next day and spent Saturday night at Jim Martin's house. Sunday, on a visit to Lee's grave with Robert and Vada Oswald, "she spilled the beans," as Robert later put it. "She was under tremendous pressure," he told me. "I knew I had to get her out of there." Her disclosure did not come as a complete surprise to Robert. He said that he hadn't trusted either Martin or Thorne since December. Just a week before Marina's graveside admission, Vada told Robert that Marina had discussed Jim Martin's sexual advances with her and confided that she felt threatened by the situation.

"You're going home to my house," Robert said to Marina at Lee's grave.

She agreed.

Next day, Vada Oswald took Marina to a doctor's appointment. Afterwards, they stopped by the Martin house to pick up the rest of her clothes and belongings. As they were preparing to depart, Marina said, Jim Martin called from his office. They discussed her decision to move out, and she made a suggestion that seemed to stun

Martin. "I told him that he and I and Wanda should get together to talk the whole affair over and that his wife should know the whole truth," Marina said. A meeting to address those issues was set for Robert and Vada's house the next day, but the Martins did not show. Marina telephoned them that night. "His wife was on the extension," she recalled, "and we had a three-way conversation. I told Martin I was ending his services as my business manager and my lover."

Earlier Wanda Martin had informed Marina that if Jim ever found another woman he loved, she would divorce him. The subject arose during their phone chat. "Wanda said she now knew that Jim loved her," Marina remembered, "and that she would not divorce him."

There was stickiness still ahead, however. Neither Jim Martin nor John Thorne would willingly back out of contracts they'd signed in December with Marina, guaranteeing them a 25 percent cut of her income from any source for the next ten years. With Robert's help, she engaged Dallas attorney William McKenzie and sued Martin and Thorne in April 1964. Three months later, Martin and Thorne walked away from the deal with a $12,500 settlement.

Marina's dalliance with Jim Martin probably damaged Ruth Paine more than anyone. She was Marina's "big sister," willing to fetch a very pregnant Marina and her daughter, June Lee, from New Orleans in the fall of 1963, then happy to let them and the new baby live with her in Irving without charge. Mrs. Paine had also found Lee the job at the book depository.

Just before Rachel's birth, Ruth donated blood at least twice, enabling Marina to qualify for a free delivery at Parkland Hospital. After the shootings, Mrs. Paine showed up with cookies, clothes, and other gifts for the girls, thinking that if anybody needed a friend just then, it was the widowed Russian girl.

In contrast to Mrs. Paine's experience, I was an unwitting beneficiary of Marina's personal and business problems. The

February 1964 press stories, which depicted her apparently fighting over money with her business partners, didn't bolster the image that her new lawyer, Bill McKenzie, had in mind for her. He wanted the world to see the young widow's compassionate side. So in early March 1964, McKenzie decided to arrange a newspaper interview in which Marina would ask for mercy for Jack Ruby, whose murder trial was underway.

As it happened, I was at the time discussing with McKenzie a possible interview with his new client. Marina's views on Ruby were one of the topics I said I'd like to explore. My broader agenda was to open a line of communication with Marina since anything she had to say would make news for a long time.

So far, she'd done a single television interview with Eddie Barker of KRLD in Dallas, which didn't work out too well because of Marina's broken English. She did acknowledge Lee's culpability in the Kennedy assassination however, an acknowledgment she would renounce many years later.

My forty-minute interview with her, published March 7, 1964, was her first unpaid print interview. Under the headline "Her Thoughts On Ruby: Marina Opposes Chair," I reported: "Marina Oswald doesn't want Jack Ruby sent to the electric chair for killing her husband, Lee Harvey Oswald."

"It was not right, what he did," she said slowly as she searched for the right words, "but I think he should be punished according to the law. I just do not believe in capital punishment."

From a news-gathering point of view, probably the second most important thing she offered was an apology for Lee. Marina said she wanted all Americans to know how "very badly" she felt about the assassination. "I am ashamed and sorry," she added.

Another time, she went into more detail about Oswald. "He had this strangeness about him," she told me. "He had strong political beliefs but rarely talked to me about them. He considered most women unable to understand or maybe to add anything to such conversation.

"He always seemed like a man deeply hurt by something," she continued, "and I always felt somewhat like a mother to him, felt I was helping him in some way. I've always thought what a shame that something or somebody had made him the way that he was. If I had met him in the United States and understood him, I probably would not have married him."

Marina blamed herself, in part, for the assassination, believing if she been more welcoming, more loving, on the night of November, 21, Lee's anger and frustration might not have boiled over as it did the next afternoon in Dealey Plaza.

The prelude to their last argument came earlier in the week when she tried to reach him at the rooming house. "Lee Oswald? No, nobody here by that name," a man said over the phone. Lee had neglected to tell her that he was Mr. O. H. Lee on North Beckley. Next day he called Marina and chewed her out for blowing his cover. She screamed back at him and hung up and then hung up three more times when he called to try to smooth over the spat. She worried about the impression Lee was making on her friend. "What will Ruth think?" she said. "What kind of nut will she think he is?"

Marina said she was surprised when Lee showed up that Thursday night instead of Friday as usual. "Then I became angry," she explained. "He knew he wasn't to come out there without Ruth's permission. And he knew he was supposed to telephone first." This argument did not seem different in tone or intensity from any of the scores of fights that the battling Oswalds constantly got into. Yet Lee seemed especially vulnerable this time. "He kept talking, kept talking, trying to make me feel sorry for him," she remembered. "He said he missed me and the children and was very lonely."

Marina only glared at her husband and would not speak. Pretty soon, Mrs. Paine drove up and noticed Lee playing with his older daughter. "Marina sat apart from him, pouting," she told me.

Marina later described the evening to the Warren Commission: "He was upset over the fact I would not answer him," she testified. "He tried to start a conversation with me several times, but I would not answer, and he said he did not want me to be angry with him because this upsets him. On that day he suggested that we rent an apartment in Dallas. He said he was tired of living alone and perhaps the reason for my being so angry was the fact that we were not living together, that if I wanted to, he would rent an apartment in Dallas tomorrow, that he didn't want me to remain with Ruth any longer but wanted me to live with him in Dallas.

"He repeated this not once but several times. But I refused. And he said that once again I preferred my friends to him and that I didn't need him." She told her husband that it was best for her to stay with Mrs. Paine in order to save money.

"What did he say to that?" Marina was asked.

"He said he would buy me a washing machine."

"And what did you say to that?"

"Thank you. That it would be better if he bought something for himself, that I would manage."

"That may have been the breaking point for Oswald," wrote William Manchester in *The Death of the President.* "He had nothing left, not even pride."

While surprised at Oswald's presence, Mrs. Paine made no particular mention of it that evening. Instead she tried and failed to draw Oswald into a conversation about President Kennedy's pending visit. He said nothing to her.

Dinner at half past six was tense. Lee, still unable to connect with Marina, watched television for a while and then ducked out into the garage where, while the women were busy with household chores, he undoubtedly disassembled the Mannlicher-Carcano for transport to the book depository next morning. When Mrs. Paine went to the garage at nine o'clock, she noticed he'd left the overhead light on.

When Marina went to bed later, she sensed that Lee was still awake but did not speak to him.

Marina did not believe there was any genuine ideological component in her husband's decision to assassinate the president. She understood that Lee had psychological, not political, problems, and probably the key impulse behind pulling the trigger was a pathological hunger to be recognized. "Sometimes he was a little bit sick," she told the Warren Commission. "He was a normal man, but sometimes people don't understand him. And sometimes I didn't know—he want to be popular, so everyone know who is Lee Harvey Oswald."

His bungled assault on General Walker had come to light in early December 1963, after Ruth Paine turned over a box of Oswald's possessions to police. The materials included an undated note to Marina, written in Russian, instructing her in what to do if he was arrested. The note assured her that he had paid the rent and utility bills. She was to send any news clippings about him to "the embassy," so they could help her. He also left a mailbox key, asked her to hold on to his personal papers, and told her to contact the American Red Cross for help if she needed it.

Confronted with the note, Marina conceded she was familiar with it and the reasons Lee wrote it. On April 10, 1963, the Oswalds were living in an apartment on Neely Street in Oak Cliff. That evening, according to Marina, Lee went out alone shortly after dinner. She thought he'd gone to his nightly typing class. But when he didn't return by ten o'clock, she grew nervous and went to the small enclosure he used as an office. There, she discovered the note.

Finally, a couple hours later, Lee came in the door panting, his clothes in disarray. "He came in all pale, and I could see he was nervous," she later told me. "I asked him where he had been, and he told me, 'I just tried to kill General Walker.'"

In fact, he had barely missed. The slug ripped through a window casing, skimmed Walker's scalp, and then tore a golf ball-size hole in the wall behind him, penetrating nine inches before coming to rest on a stack of pamphlets in the adjoining room.

"Who is General Walker?" Marina asked. "Does he have a wife and family?"

"He's a fascist," Lee snapped back.

According to Marina, Lee later told her he had planned the shooting for two months. He showed her a notebook with photos of the Walker house in the exclusive Turtle Creek area of Dallas and a map to help him find the residence.

A source I developed on the Warren Commission added a bit more to the story. He told me that after that night, Marina apparently used the Russian-language note Oswald left her as leverage. Whenever Lee started to abuse her, Marina mentioned the letter and scared him into worrying that she'd turn him in, and therefore he left her alone.

The tale of Oswald's second alleged target that April is somewhat murkier. On January 13, 1964, Jim Martin informed Robert Oswald that Marina had recently told him that Lee threatened to shoot former Vice President Richard Nixon. On February 20, Robert told the Warren Commission, "He said Marina had locked Lee in the bathroom for the entire day." According to Robert's diary, Marina also confirmed the story to him, once again in conjunction with a trip to the cemetery.

"We had been talking about the children," Robert testified. "And at a pause in this conversation, she started relating to me this incident. 'Robert, Lee also wanted to shoot Mr. Nixon', she told me. I replied, 'Yes, Jim told me about this when we were sitting in the den that afternoon.'"

Marina explained to Robert that Lee had been angry but calmed down after his stay in the bathroom. Warren Commission assistant counsel Alfred Jenner was incredulous. "Did it occur to you that it might be quite difficult for a ninety-eight-pound woman to lock your brother in a bathroom?"

"Yes, sir," Robert answered, "it has occurred to me exactly how this is possible, to an extent that a bathroom usually has a lock on the inside and not on the outside."

Marina later repeated the story in general to me but not the stuff about locking Lee in the bathroom. This public disclosure got her into trouble. Back in February when she testified before the

Warren Commission about the General Walker episode, commission member John Sherman Cooper, a Republican senator from Kentucky, asked her, "Did he express to you any hostility toward any particular official of the United States?"

Marina said no.

I don't know whether the commission members simply overlooked Robert Oswald's later testimony on the subject, but they made a lot of threatening sounds and recalled Marina to Washington for further testimony after my story appeared on June 12.

Marina was furious with me. "What do you know about all this?" she demanded over the phone. "You have caused me hurt! Caused me to have government people calling me a liar! Do you know what you've done? Isn't anything private?"

I began to speak but then thought better of it.

"Think of my children! Your story is wrong."

I asked her what part was wrong.

"The whole thing! And the way you slanted at me as if I was a criminal." Then she hung up.

The story was absolutely accurate, and when she reappeared before the commission that month, the mood was not warm. Marina was asked why she hadn't mentioned the Nixon story in February. "There were an awful lot of questions at that time," she answered. "And I was very tired, and I felt that I had told everything. And I don't remember. I can't understand why I didn't mention this. It would have been better for me to mention it the first time than to make you all do more work on it." She told the committee that Lee came in the apartment dressed in his suit and said, "Today, Nixon is coming. I want to go out and have a look at him."

"I know how you look," Marina remembered replying. "You have already promised me not to play anymore with that thing," meaning the handgun Oswald carried. She testified that they argued for perhaps a half hour before her husband finally left.

"I am going to go out and find out if there will be an appropriate opportunity," he said, "and if there is, I will use the pistol."

"Didn't that statement he made about Vice President Nixon make a strong impression on you?" asked Allen Dulles.

"I don't know," Marina answered. "I was pregnant at the time. I had a lot of other things to worry about. I was getting pretty well tired of all these escapades of his."

CHAPTER ELEVEN

Marina Gets Even with Tabloids

There have been four occasions in my professional life when government officials wanted to know what I knew, but I wouldn't tell them, so they tapped my phone. I don't think these measures were ever justified, and I also doubt that it was ever worth their trouble.

The first time I suspected that my phone was tapped was in late June of 1964 after I had obtained, in April, what Lee Harvey Oswald called his "Historic Diary," otherwise known as his Russian diary, together with a number of his personal effects, photos, and documents.

The diary, about five thousand handwritten words in all, covered his life from October 16, 1959, the day he arrived in the Soviet Union, to March 27, 1962, just after he and Marina flew with one-month-old June Lee from Minsk to Dallas.

Of course, the diary was a major newsbreak. Accordingly I went to great pains and personal expense to authenticate it. Also the fact that Oswald was highly critical of the USSR raised the possibility that some of his Russian friends mentioned in its pages might suffer Soviet retribution if we repeated their names in print.

So I went to Ilya Mamantov, a Russian-born research geologist and friend of mine then teaching at SMU. Ilya, prominent in the Dallas Russian émigré community, had provided the translation when the Dallas police brought Marina Oswald to headquarters for questioning on the afternoon of the assassination.

Ilya looked at the diary and said, in his view, some of Oswald's friends in Minsk might indeed have trouble with the authorities if we identified them in the paper. At my request, Mamantov then telephoned several of these people, who confirmed his misgivings. As a consequence, we withheld their names.

The story of Oswald's diary ran on page one of practically every American daily—and overseas papers as well. This was our first-day headline:

SECRET DIARY

OSWALD'S THOUGHTS BARED

Among our many disclosures, we told the world that Oswald claimed to have been on the Soviet secret police payroll. "When I went to Russia in the winter of 1959, my funds were very limited," he wrote. "So after a certain time, after the Russians had assured themselves that I was really the naïve American who believed in communism, they arranged for me to receive a certain amount of money every month. Oh, it came technically through the Red Cross as financial help to a poor political immigrant, but it was arranged by the MVD [Ministry of Internal Affairs]." He reported that once he lost faith in communist society and started to negotiate his exit from the Soviet Union "my 'Red Cross' allotment was cut off."

Early in the diary, he also described his attempted suicide when he believed he would not be allowed to stay in the country. "7:00 p.m. I decide to end it. Soak wrist in cold water to numb the pain. Then slash my left wrist. Then place into bathtub of hot water." Rimma Sherikova, Oswald's Intourist guide, discovered him on the bathroom floor and summoned an ambulance, which rushed Oswald to the hospital, where five stiches were taken in his left wrist.

The diary's publication caught everybody by surprise, and there were a number of people who were very angry with me. The FBI was quickly dispatched to find out where I got the material and, if possible, whether more was coming. "An embarrassment," commission member and former CIA Director Allen Dulles later told me. "If the lawyers could have gotten hold of you," Dulles added, "I hesitate to think what might have become of you." He told me the publication of the diary hadn't bothered him personally. "You just released the facts," Dulles explained, "You didn't attempt to color it as some would have done."

J. Edgar Hoover took a dimmer view of my work. Within hours of the first story's appearance on Saturday, June 27, 1964, Hoover ordered Gordon Shanklin to sniff out the leak. Shanklin dispatched two agents to interview me several times. They also questioned several editors at the *News*, to whom I had not disclosed my source's identity. I knew better.

Ted Dealey called me from his office after the agents departed. "The FBI just left my office trying to get me to tell them where you got Oswald's diary," he growled. "I told them I wasn't going to tell them anything, and I showed them the way to the newsroom and told them they could interview you. They'll be there momentarily. I hope you don't tell them a damned thing either."

Minutes later Johnny King swung by my desk, wearing a large grin. "May I present these two men from the FBI," King said. "They think you might have some business with them." He introduced Special Agent Manny Clements and another agent whose name I have forgotten, then moved off a few feet—close enough to monitor the conversation but not close enough to be part of an arrest.

"We'd like for you to tell us where you obtained the Russian diary," Agent Clements began in a friendly manner as he and his partner pulled up a couple of reporters' chairs close to my messy workplace. "You see, to you this is just a news story," he went on, "but to us it's much more. Somebody is leaking material that shouldn't be released. We've got to find out who is dealing in this material and why."

"You sound like you think I bribed somebody to get into the commission archives," I replied. "Or that somebody is selling this information. I don't like that perception. It's totally untrue."

We parried in this way for a few minutes to nobody's advantage. I told them that I expected to work as a journalist the rest of my life. To divulge information could—undoubtedly would—be detrimental to my source or sources and was not something I would ever do.

Clements said something like, "Well, we intend to find out."

I answered "Good luck," or whatever, and the interview ended.

The magnitude of the story—the *News* fielded at least seventy-five queries from all over the world from publications asking if there was more to come, could they reprint the entire piece, and so forth. It caused some uproar in the newsroom. I was disappointed in a couple of my colleagues when they warned that my life would never be the same if I didn't cooperate and tell the FBI everything. My only answer was that my life would never be the same if I did. I have never ratted out my sources.

The best advice came from Harry McCormick. "Listen, Kissy,"—I don't know where Harry came up with that nickname, which he used with a half dozen or so young reporters—"don't tell 'em anything. They don't really expect you to tell 'em." Harry did warn me that I could expect a tap on my phone. "They've already been embarrassed enough by the assassination," he said. "They won't want to admit they can't find out where a reporter scooped them. But don't say anything on your phone for a few days that you wouldn't want to become a part of a report somewhere down the line."

The next afternoon I received another call from Manny Clements. "You ready to tell us now?" he asked.

"No, nothing has changed."

"Well, if you're going to be in tomorrow morning, I'd like to run something by you. Eleven o'clock agreeable?"

That night I was discussing the bureau probe with my wife when suddenly I had an inspiration. "I'll call you tomorrow morning as soon as I get to the office," I told her, "and I'll set a trap for them. If the FBI is listening, I'll know it when they come by at eleven."

"You're going to get in deeper trouble," she warned me.

Possibly, but this was the fun part. At the office next morning I telephoned home, ostensibly to discuss my concerns over the FBI investigations. "I'm a little worried they are going to find out where I got the diary," I said gravely, "that Shanklin slipped it to me. He could lose his job."

Now all I had to do was wait. A short time later Clements and his partner reappeared at the paper. Manny tried as usual to be friendly, persuasive. "We don't want to hurt anybody here," he said, "but just like you, we have a job to do. We know where the diary is and how many copies are available and where they are. All we need to know is where you obtained your copy."

Then he tipped his hand. "What we are seriously concerned about is that somebody official is involved here."

I stifled a smirk.

"Can we be reasonably assured that nobody in the U.S. Attorney's office gave you this material? Can you assure us nobody employed by the Federal Bureau of Investigation allowed you to see it or copy it?"

"Sorry," I said, absolutely delighted with myself and my little stratagem. I imagined Gordon Shanklin with steam coming out his ears. "But I am not going to exclude anybody. What you have to do is your job and what I must do is mine. I am not going to tell you."

Manny's partner stooped to intimidation. "You familiar with federal grand juries?" he snarled at me as they left.

Afterward crusty old Ted Dealey summoned me up to the executive floor and shook my hand. "Damn fine job, Hugh. Glad you didn't break down and tell 'em.

"They won't be forgetting your name soon around here, young man," he added.

Two years later, when he presented a five-year service pin to me, Dealey called me Frank Reece.

Actually, for all his tough talk and bluster, Dealey was fairly easily panicked. Following the paper's first two installments of Oswald's diary, Dallas lawyer William McKenzie threatened a lawsuit against the *News* on Marina's behalf. When it appeared that the mere chance of being sued might scuttle our third and final installment, I lit a back fire, telling my editors that the *Detroit Free Press* had gotten hold of the material and was poised to scoop our scoop. This of course was not true, but it did persuade the *News* to proceed with the third article.

⚜

I was briefly popular with a number of large news-gathering operations interested in acquiring copies of my files, from which to produce their own diary stories. Prominent among them was *Life* magazine, which promised to put the diary story on their cover if I chose them. *Life*'s Dallas bureau chief, Holland McCombs, was an old friend and trusted colleague. I told Holland that if I could arrange it I would allow *Life* to have the material on an exclusive basis.

The *News* understandably frowned on staff reporters selling their work in this way unless permission to make such a deal was granted in advance. So I went to the managing editor, Jack Krueger, to ask for his blessing and guidance. He took a couple days to think about it and then called me into his office to offer a suggestion. "Why don't you have your wife sell it to *Life*?" Krueger suggested. "That way, technically you haven't broken the rules. But keep me in the loop please."

Life had deep pockets. However, if I had wanted to hit the jackpot, I could have taken any of several lucrative offers I'd already received from book publishers. My only real concern was to recoup the approximately $2,500 of my own money I'd spent on researching and reporting the story. If anyone actually owned the diary, I believed, it probably was Marina.

I told McCombs I'd take a check to cover my expenses, made out to my wife, and he agreed. He also agreed to protect the identities of Oswald's friends in Minsk and promised that the *News* would be credited in the magazine as the source of the story.

Life did change some names, as agreed, but did not credit us. Even though Holland was a close friend of Time, Inc. founder, Henry Luce, once the *Life* editors had my reporting and documentation in hand, they failed to honor their promise to say where they got it. At my urging they did negotiate a purchase price for the material with Marina, who received $20,000.

— ⚜ —

In October 1964, I undid any good will Marina bore me with a front-page story I wrote for the *New York Journal-American* that mentioned her heavy smoking and drinking. A television reporter once told me he watched Marina finish off a fifth of Bailey's Bristol Crème, washing the stuff down with beer, in two hours "and still she didn't seem drunk!" My article also described how Marina had become "very Americanized" in the savvy way she peddled interviews and the *Life* material.

Then on June 1, 1965, I got a tip she was to be married to Kenneth Porter, a foreman at Texas Instruments. Photographer Bill Winfrey and I chased the couple north across the Oklahoma border to the little town of Durant, where there was no wait to be wed. Winfrey and I lost Kenneth's car in Durant momentarily and then found ourselves at a stop light right next to the two lovebirds. Once Marina saw me, she had Kenneth veer quickly to the right, and we lost them again. They did not get married in the Oklahoma town. Instead they veered back toward Dallas to the farm community of Fate, Texas, where an obliging justice of the peace interrupted his plowing to pronounce them man and wife.

—❈❈❈—

Upon her marriage to Porter, Marina fashioned a domestic life for herself of relative tranquility as a wife and mom in Rockwall, a little town east of Dallas. Almost all requests for interviews, or even comment, were firmly turned down.

Such was the situation confronting Mike Cochran of the AP in this period when he was instructed to produce an assassination anniversary story, a familiar assignment in Texas. His editors wanted the piece to include an interview with Marina. The probability of scoring such a sit-down seemed remote to Cochran, who nonetheless drove out to the Porter residence at a time of day when he could be reasonably certain that Kenneth Porter was at work. "He already had driven off one reporter with a pistol," Cochran told me, "and I didn't want any of that."

Marina answered the door. Cochran introduced himself. She immediately cut him off. "No interview," she said, twice.

He was at a loss, unusual for a reporter of his caliber. "But," he remembered, "I must have had a funny expression on my face or something because she said, 'Is something wrong?'"

Searching for a coherent reply, he finally blurted, "Well, Marina, I haven't seen you since Lee's burial. I was a pallbearer and..."

She smiled. "You were a pallbearer for Lee? Well, then, the least I can do is invite you in for coffee."

To his delight, they talked for hours, drinking coffee and smoking together. To his distress, he didn't know what if anything Marina said was on the record. He kept thinking of pulling out his notebook but thought better of it lest she terminate their chat at the sight of it.

Finally Marina rose and fetched a magazine. "Read this and see what you think," she said, opening it to an article about her, written by some doctor or social scientist. Cochran recalls that the piece argued "she was actually at fault for JFK's death because of her sexual rejection of Oswald the night before."

"I think he's right," Marina said as he put down the magazine. Now his dilemma was acute. Not only had Marina spoken to him, but she'd made a headline-grabbing assertion of personal responsibility for the president's death. But how to get it into print?

He cast his eyes around the room, trying to think of something, when he noticed an unusual-looking set of andirons resting on the floor near, not in, the fireplace. "I think those are the most unusual fireplace decorations I've ever seen," he said, lamely.

"Oh, my gosh!" Marina replied. "Those are the ugliest I've ever had in my house." She said her husband had bought them and then looked straight at the AP reporter. "You can't put that in your story," she said. "That's one thing you can't write."

No problem, ma'am.

Cochran, ecstatic, considered that Marina had just put everything else she'd said on the record, a reporting coup of the first order. "I got out of there as fast as I could," he told me. "I drove a few blocks away and parked and began writing down quotes."

He wrote up his anniversary story for the Sunday papers, of course leading with Marina's remarks, filed it, and then caught a plane for California and a journalism conference there. His return flight on Sunday afternoon stopped in Lubbock, giving him just enough time to rush inside the terminal to buy a copy of the local *Avalanche-Journal*, fully expecting to see his big story featured on the front page. When he finally found it buried inside, all mention of Marina accepting blame for November 22 had been edited out. As soon as he could get to a phone, Mike called Bob Johnson, the AP editor in Dallas.

"I know why you're calling," said Johnson, who then explained why his big scoop had been axed. The AP, he reminded Cochran, was then facing a libel suit filed by General Walker. When top executives in New York read Marina's admissions, they feared that she too would sue. Rather than risk more litigation, they simply killed her quotes.

Cochran was naturally annoyed, then vindicated—sort of—a quarter century later when, as he once again interviewed Marina, he asked her if she remembered the magazine story and the author's opinions of her culpability in the assassination.

She said she didn't, then added at once, "But I don't deny it."

Older and wiser, Cochran tucked the quote deep into the story—and this time it survived.

***

After my *Journal-American* article of 1964, Marina regarded me as her enemy until a scurrilous tabloid article served to rehabilitate me in her eyes. From time to time over the years, she met with conspiracy buffs, some of whom took advantage of her. At last—and who knows why—she announced that her slain husband hadn't killed anyone. I tried to get in touch with her a couple of times during this period, but Marina told me she had nothing to say to me.

Then, after a silence of more than a decade, my telephone rang one morning, and there she was.

"Is this Hugh Aynesworth, my enemy?"

"Well, it's me, Marina," I replied. "But I'm not your enemy. How are you?"

She went straight to the point.

"Do you read the *National Enquirer*?"

"Not if I can avoid it."

"Well please get one and read a story in this edition. It's about me and the children, and it's really horrible for them. I need your help. I have nobody else to turn to."

I figured that must be so, given her deep dislike for me. I was curious to see what kind of article it took for Marina Oswald Porter to reach out to me for help, so I went to the grocery store, bought the *Enquirer*, and immediately understood why she was so upset. It was a really nasty piece of work, purporting to tell how June Lee and Rachel were hated and taunted in their neighborhood.

This was not the picture I'd received over the years. From all reports, Marina and Ken Porter had been great parents, and the girls were doing extremely well, especially in view of the past. I called Marina back and emphatically recommended that she sue the *Enquirer*.

"I can't afford a lawyer," she said. "Do you know anyone?"

"Not many that know libel law well," I said, "but give me a few hours to check around."

My choice was Frank Jackson, a former NFL running back who'd played for the Kansas City Chiefs and Miami Dolphins and now practiced criminal defense law in Dallas with great success.

"I'll do what I can," Frank said when I explained the situation. That turned out to be quite a lot. Jackson determined that Marguerite was partly behind the mischief. She had helped plant the story through a friend who had neither met nor even seen her grandchildren. In the end, the *Enquirer* settled for more than $50,000, most of which I hoped would be put away for June Lee and Rachel's college educations.

Marina graciously thanked me for my help and asked me to lunch with her daughters. We spoke warmly, like old friends, not enemies. A year or so later, however, when I called to ask for a comment on an aspect of the assassination story, she told me she was under contract and could not be quoted.

In 1989, Marina finally became a naturalized citizen. Seven years later, she delighted a certain subset of conspiracy buffs by declaring on *Oprah* that she now disbelieved that Lee had shot anyone back in 1963. Robert Oswald, by contrast, has never doubted his brother's responsibility for both the Kennedy and the Tippit killings. A short while later, when I asked her over the telephone about her change of heart, she said, "It's just too much. As much as I believed he *must* have done it, I have been given so much evidence that he couldn't have done it."

There was no point in asking just what evidence she had in mind. If it existed, much of the world and I already knew about it and had not been similarly persuaded by it. Moreover she was a mother with two children who'd been alive on November 22, 1963. They had suffered considerable indignities and abuse over the ensuing decades and would surely have been thrilled to believe their father was an innocent man.

She told me she'd heard nothing of, or from, her onetime lover, Jim Martin. Nor had there been any contact with Ruth Paine, who had done so much to help and protect Marina through her trying early months in the United States. It seemed that Mrs. Paine had been discarded once she was of no further utility to Marina. "What would we have to talk about?" she asked.

Marina retired a few years ago but kept in touch with several conspiracy theorists over the years since a bevy of them had convinced her that Lee was actually innocent. I spoke with her occasionally, phoning about various things. A few opportunists asked me for her telephone number, but I never shared it.

In 2006 I received a call from a friend in Fort Worth who worked at Texas Christian University. David Murph asked if I knew where Marina was. "I've got a rather interesting situation here, one that I think she might be interested in," he added. Then he told me a bizarre story.

A Fort Worth lawyer, Forrest Marquart, had suffered from Alzheimer's and retired, leaving a few file cabinets full of his records and materials. The firm leaders who cleaned out these cabinets found an interesting item: a small gold wedding ring with Russian script inside. His friends recalled that the lawyer had once represented Marina and thought maybe Marina had given the ring to Mr. Marquart years before. "They want to get it to the rightful owner," Murph told me, "but they aren't sure what to do."

I called Mrs. Ruth Paine, whose name was mentioned in some of the papers accompanying the ring, but she didn't have any idea how it had ended up in Mr. Marquart's file cabinet. Then I called Dr. Linda Norton, a forensic psychologist who had headed the team that exhumed Oswald's body in the early 1980s, but she could shed no light on the matter either. A lengthy article I wrote in the *Washington Times* failed to turn up any other leads.

I contacted Marina, who was living in Fate, Texas, an hour east of Dallas, because I figured the ring was rightfully hers. She said she didn't recall the lawyer or the ring and vowed she didn't want any part of it. I then called Lee's brother, Robert, in Wichita Falls. "I have no idea how it got there or why," he said, "but yes, I'd love to have it."

I suggested that the law firm donate the ring to the Sixth Floor Museum at Dealey Plaza—the fine institution that has accumulated quite a JFK collection. Luke Ellis, one of the law firm's partners, met with Nicola Longford, the museum's executive director, but the museum refused to accept it because, officials said, there was no clear indication of ownership.

But, just last December, Marina, a daughter, and son-in-law, met with the law firm and took possession of the ring. Marina told me earlier this year that she had placed it with an auction house in the Northeast, with a September date for its sale. "Some people have told me it might bring quite a lot," she said, "but I don't know. People tell you things, you know."

CHAPTER TWELVE

"This Guy Was Crazy": Dr. Beavers

Jack Ruby was the quintessential nowhere man. He even resembled the Beatles' cartoon creation. Full of big stories, bigger dreams, and braggadocio, the strip show operator was first and foremost a low life, a man who searched for class as though he understood the concept.

Often he would tell his pals that someday he'd have a club in Las Vegas. That, to Ruby, was class. He told his lawyer, Stanley Kaufman, that when he made it big in Sin City, he wouldn't have to worry any more about years and years of difficulties with the Internal Revenue Service. "He said, 'They never bother the big, important guys. You don't see guys hassled once they become somebody in show business,'" Kaufman recalled.

Hardly a week went by in Dallas when you wouldn't see Ruby promoting some inane product, chasing fire trucks, pushing himself into public displays, or passing out his Carousel Club calling cards at boxing matches, in the bars, or on downtown streets. One time he might be promoting a young black singer and dancer, another time an exercise board, or some sort of snake oil "sure to make you thinner and more powerful." Once he touted a gangly Arkansas girl as a "dancer," predicting she would be a smash hit at the Carousel. "She'll be the only Jewish stripper Dallas has ever seen," he told Don Campbell, the *News* ad executive. The girl never graced his stage.

Ruby never married. He was somewhat of a health nut, and I never found a person who recalled him taking a drink of alcohol. Because he was at times almost prissy and had a very slight lisp, some thought he was homosexual. For several years, he dated a shy, pretty woman named Alice Nichols, but by November 1963, they hadn't been together in months. Their usual dates, only periodic, meant dinner and a movie. Mrs. Nichols testified briefly at his trial but then faded into obscurity as the media, showing more sensitivity than usual, left her alone.

Even those who should have known him well often admitted they didn't. "He had this big, big heart," said sister Eva. His sister Eileen Kaminsky once described him to me as "this great big puppy dog. He might slobber all over you, but you couldn't dislike him."

Fact was, I—and many others—disliked him intensely.

Bob Larkin, once Ruby's bouncer and later a club owner on his own, said that while Jack could act warmhearted toward many, he had a "weird, unusual" bent. Larkin said that one time he was stabbed in the stomach and writhing on the sidewalk—not dangerously injured but in a lot of pain—when Ruby walked up to him.

He said Ruby kicked him. "And kept saying, 'Get up, Bob. Get up.'"

Melvin Belli, during his first weeks as Ruby's lawyer, got in trouble with the local bar association—and the Ruby family—for describing his client as "a Damon Runyon character, a scrounger with a million and one different ventures. He builds up in his own mind all sorts of grandiose ideas."

Carl Freund, a prolific contributor at the *News* and a fast writer, stepped into the same critical role that Paul Crume had played on November 22 in the paper's handling of the assassination story. Freund processed and fine-tuned reportage from several reporters handling various aspects of Ruby's burst into infamy that Sunday.

Carl dropped by my desk the following morning to apologize for not using more of my file in the November twenty-fifth story. As we spoke, another reporter came by, Freund's story in hand. "Look at this," he grinned as he tossed down the newspaper and walked away.

Freund looked and read a little bit—then it hit him. The headline read, "Nightclub Man Takes Roll of Executioner."

I had not noticed the misspelling of *role*, nor had anyone else that I saw that morning.

As the ambulance rushed the expiring Lee Harvey Oswald off to Parkland, a number of reporters, me included, headed upstairs at City Hall to ferret out what details of the story we could. There wasn't much to learn at first, but several of us noted a small-time local defense lawyer named Tom Howard arriving for a meeting with Ruby's sister, Eva Grant, and one other person I couldn't identify.

Jim Underwood, a KRLD reporter, was greeted warmly by Eva, and I think he was privy to the brief meeting they had in a police station anteroom that afternoon. I don't think they met with Ruby himself at that time, but I am not sure.

A short while later, as Howard headed back to his office directly across Akard Street, several of us trailed him. "Are you gonna plead insanity?" one newsman shouted.

Howard stopped, smiled at us, and replied, "Well, I guess you'd say that anybody who'd kill a man in the police station might just be crazy, but that's something we will have to decide at a later point." Tom, a country-talkin' good ol' boy popular with the courthouse guys, said he had to talk with family members and would be glad to answer questions, possibly later that day.

After a few minutes, the other reporters peeled off in search of better copy, but I had noticed that the last person out of Howard's office had left the door slightly ajar. After waiting for what seemed an eternity (but was probably four or five minutes) and when I could be sure none of the other reporters could see me, I slipped inside.

It was late afternoon on Sunday. There were no secretaries. The lights were dimmed. I didn't see anyone in the office, but I heard voices—Howard's and others—on the other side of an office wall. Someone said, "Well, hell, just call him," and they chatted a moment or two about how to approach whomever they were planning to call. I heard Eva say, "Well, tell him right off, we don't have any money."

They put the call through, and I heard a telephone click on a receptionist's desk near me, which gave me an idea. Maybe I could ease the receiver off the hook—they were big, black and heavy then— and find out who was on the other end.

I hesitated, scared to death somebody would bolt out of Howard's office and catch me. Still I needed to know what was happening. Knowing and understanding defense lawyers even then, I knew that if I waited for an explanation, it might never be forthcoming, and if it was, it would be twisted to benefit the client.

Though I could hear Howard's booming voice, I still needed the other side of that conversation. Just behind that desk was another office. I had already been through so much emotionally that weekend, I doubt I consciously considered what might happen if I got caught. I just sidled into the office, slowly lifted the receiver, and listened. Unlike two days before, when I had stumbled on the scene with no paper to write on, this time I had several index cards stuffed in my pocket.

I heard a woman saying, "Oh, here he is, hold on a minute." Then boomed a deep, drawling voice I thought I recognized. A couple of comments later, I was sure. It was Percy Foreman—undoubtedly the most famous criminal lawyer in Texas history, an old-time orator and spellbinder. Percy had won something like three hundred straight murder cases.

I had known him only casually but had heard a thousand tales of how Foreman was so good that sometimes prosecutors tried to avoid trying cases against him. His presence in a case—always expensive—usually changed many aspects of a murder trial. He was said to be absolutely phenomenal at jury selection, which he later told me was "more than half the battle."

They began to discuss a possible insanity plea for Ruby. "You've got to build a strong case—believable witnesses who will say this man was so upset at Kennedy's killing that he couldn't operate normally," Foreman suggested. "Hell, everybody in the country was upset. I was. Weren't you, Tom? Now if it was me trying this—"

Howard cut him off. "Percy," he said, "that's why I'm calling you. The family wants you to help us, to help me."

A man I had never seen before, possibly one of Howard's law partners, swept out from behind the closed door and hurried down to a restroom on the south side of the offices. I jumped just in time, slipping under the desk. It seemed a lifetime until I heard the man walk back in and close the door.

I was really afraid. I knew that if the session in Howard's office ended abruptly, I was done for. They'd be visiting me down the row from Jack Ruby. But the temptation was too great. I needed to know if Foreman was going to represent Ruby. I needed to know how much money he was going to charge. I needed to know so many things— things nobody else in the media would know.

I had stopped sweating, and I eased the receiver up again. This time an agitated male with a Midwestern accent was almost screaming, "I don't care what he wants! Don't deal with the son of a bitch one more minute!"

"I'll be there as soon as I can," he continued. "You see that he's treated okay and look after Eva."

I quickly hung up the phone and crept out into the later afternoon. I ran back across the street to City Hall and called the newspaper office. One of the assistant city editors asked me if I had filed my first-person stuff from seeing Ruby shoot Oswald, and I said I had called in hours before. "Well, I don't see it anywhere," he told me. "Better come on in and make sure we have it all."

It was several weeks before I got the entire story of those phone conversations in Howard's office. The shouting Midwesterner turned out to be Jack's brother Earl in Detroit, who owned a thriving cleaning establishment in Detroit's Cobo Hall. Earl would bankroll Jack's defense.

As the phone call suggested, Earl instantly disliked Foreman, not least because the Houston lawyer was asking for a $75,000 guarantee before getting involved. Concerned about Howard's judgment in even soliciting Foreman's opinions, Earl immediately flew to California, where he watched Melvin Belli in trial. Within hours, he hired the flamboyant Belli to represent Jack.

When Belli arrived in Dallas with his longtime pal Joe Tonahill of Jasper, Texas, in tow, it was just a matter of time before Howard was scuttled. "I would have put Jack on the stand and gotten him to tell the jury how he felt, how he hurt, how he bled when that communist killed our president," Howard told reporters after he was replaced. "I know enough about Jack Ruby that he would have cried, wailed, blubbered all over himself. They couldn't have put a man like this to death. After all, how many of them [jurors] might have felt the same way?"

Howard wasn't the only one who believed that this strategy might have worked. "If they had moved the trial out of Dallas, we could have come close to walking him," Foreman later told me. When the family finally hired him as an appeals expert in late 1964, Foreman didn't last long. He and Earl still couldn't abide each other. Foreman said he finally quit because "the family can't agree on anything."

But back to Belli. Though he was a wonderfully adept personal injury lawyer, the San Francisco attorney had never mounted a homicide defense. He was a flashy dresser, quick with a quip, and vicious in his criticism, which he often aimed at Dallas authorities and the *News*. From the moment Belli hit town and Bill Alexander laughed publicly at his fur-lined briefcase, it was all about the courthouse crowd making fun of the silver-haired interloper while Belli daily berated the *News*, the city itself, and all it stood for.

The Dallas establishment found much to dislike in Belli. Though there were plenty of Dallasites who patently deserved comeuppance for their primitive social and political biases, most citizens reasonably considered themselves fair and open minded. Belli didn't wear well with them.

"If he had been able to get a change of venue, all this folderol might have been of value," said Charles Tessmer, one of Dallas's most talented criminal lawyers, "but when poor Jack had to face a jury that had already endured weeks of taunting, anti-Dallas rhetoric, there was no way he would win. Of course, that defense didn't help much either."

District Judge Joe B. Brown was a friendly, outgoing character, a man who liked the press—that is, until he took a harsh dose of out-of-town media abuse, some deserved, most not. Belli, behind his back, used to chortle and call the judge "Necessity." Asked why he called Brown that, Belli would slap his leg and drop his punch line, "Because necessity knows no law."

Brown decided early on he wasn't going to allow a defense move to take the trial elsewhere. That was apparent by his rulings in a change of venue hearing. I once asked him if he didn't think it would be better for all—what naiveté!—if he moved the trial somewhere else in Texas.

"Where the hell else?" Brown snapped. "Everybody in Texas saw what he did. Everybody in the world had seen it ten times since then. A change of venue is for when they can assure a jury panel would not be tainted by publicity or intense prejudice. This case doesn't qualify."

A few days later Brown called me into his chambers at a noon break and told me with a big smile: "Hey, I found the perfect place."

Sensing I did not understand, he said, "the place to move to the trial to, you know."

"Yeah," he continued, "it's Mentone, Texas. There are only fifty-one people in the whole county, and only two of 'em have television sets."

I wasn't sure where he was heading.

"But where in hell would I sequester the jury?" he laughed as we walked out together.

When Judge Brown ruled that the trial would remain in Dallas, Belli finally began to devise a defense. Joe Tonahill told me in 1999 that the California lawyer was so certain he would be able to obtain a change of venue that little had been done to build a secondary line of defense.

Within a few weeks, the Ruby family in particular became extremely worried. "I don't know what they're doing," Earl told me one afternoon. "They meet and eat and drink and spend money, but here it is nine days before trial, and Belli won't even tell me what witnesses he wants to use and when he wants them to testify."

Unbeknown to brother Earl, Belli and Tonahill hoped to convince jurors that Ruby was unable to control his impulses that morning in the police basement. They called it the "psychomotor epilepsy" defense, and it originated late one evening as Belli and some of the national media guys who regularly partied with the defense were whooping it up at the Statler Hilton Hotel. The famous Bob Considine of the *Journal American* later said that his colleague, star columnist Dorothy Kilgallen, was at the gathering.

"She said Belli and a couple others were closely examining various pictures of Ruby in their suite," Considine recounted, "when Belli noted something he thought strange about the Bob Jackson photo (the one that showed Oswald grimacing as he was shot). Dorothy said Belli leaped up and said, 'By God! That's it. That's it!'"

Belli later confirmed to me this indeed was the moment he first noticed that Ruby pulled the trigger on his black Colt .38 with his middle finger, instead of his forefinger. That gave Belli his idea. The use of the middle finger was a symptom of a mental disorder, he decided.

Thus was born the psychomotor epilepsy defense.

Then, since he was unaware of anybody who had ever used that tactic in a murder defense, Belli had to hustle to find expert witnesses to explain the defense to the jury.

The next few days were frantic for both sides. Belli collected a powerful team of psychiatric experts—persons who would testify that Ruby seemed to have suffered a momentary lapse of some sort, psychomotor epilepsy perhaps. Henry Wade and Bill Alexander hit the books on the subject and contacted every expert they could find to rebut Belli's team.

Ruby's defense hung on the expert testimony of a University of Texas psychiatrist, Dr. Martin Towler, and a Baltimore psychiatric legend, Dr. Manfred Guttmacher. Towler testified strongly that Ruby had been in a seizure mode and said a person in the midst of such a seizure would move like an automaton, oblivious to what he was doing. He suggested that the scores of brawls that Ruby had been involved in over the years—especially when he had been hit in the head—could have caused irreparable brain damage. He described it as "a seizure disorder" and later said, "It falls into the category of a psychomotor variant."

Guttmacher, who had written several books on various forms of psychiatric abnormality, said Ruby was under some sort of extreme strain, but he ruled out schizophrenia or paranoia. Ruby, he testified, seemed "unable to tolerate anxiety" and was "a very unstable individual."

Belli tried to steer Guttmacher to use the phrase "psychomotor epilepsy," but the Baltimore doctor wouldn't. As John Kaplan and Jon R. Waltz observed in their book, *The Trial of Jack Ruby*, "No matter how hard Belli had tried through his questioning to force the witness to hew to the defense's preordained line, psychomotor epilepsy had gotten lost. The jurors would soon know, if they did not already realize, that the defense's chief attorney and his principal expert had passed like ships in the night."

We later learned why Belli and Guttmacher were so clearly at odds. Guttmacher had delivered a memo to Belli on March 3, the day the twelfth juror was chosen. He told Belli he couldn't testify for certain that Ruby had suffered a psychotic break at the time he killed Oswald.

Unfortunately for the psychomotor epilepsy defense, it was too late for Belli to go shopping for another expert.

Guttmacher later told reporters in Baltimore he was discouraged at how Belli used him and complained that he seldom had a chance to explain anything pertinent in his testimony. Belli, claimed Guttmacher, "surrounded himself with all sorts of characters, even a movie crew. They were actually filming how he tried the case. He was never available to me."

Tonahill, in a rare moment of reflection about his friend Belli, told me in 1999 that though he hated to admit it, the defense's psychiatric witnesses had been somewhat negated by the preparation done by the DA's office. "Henry, and even more so, Alexander, had really done their homework," Tonahill said.

In the end, it didn't matter whether Jack Ruby was a fool, a man stricken with a sudden urge to kill, or a demonic wannabe who thought he might end up a hero. Technically he died an innocent man. The jurors convicted Ruby and agreed that he should die for shooting Lee Harvey Oswald. But the Texas Court of Criminal Appeals reversed that judgment, and a new trial was scheduled for Wichita Falls.

Ruby's death from cancer intervened.

Though the failure to take the trial to another city was mentioned as one of two main reasons the judgment was overturned, the most damning reason was that the appeals judges did not believe the testimony of one Dallas cop—the man who gave the jury a reason to believe that Ruby's act was not a sudden urge but something he'd considered for two days.

On Friday, March 6, 1964, the final day of the prosecution's case, Sergeant Patrick Dean "stunned the courtroom," as Bob Fenley and Jim Lehrer reported in the *Times Herald*, "when he said the nightclub owner told him he thought of killing Oswald when he noticed the 'sarcastic sneer' on the accused assassin's face."

Fenley and Lehrer continued, "Over strenuous defense objections, the officer related his conversation with Ruby in the fifth floor city jail approximately ten minutes after Oswald was shot. 'He said something to the effect he had thought about this two nights prior when he saw him—Oswald—on the show-up stand,' the officer related. Sergeant Dean said Ruby told him he 'wanted the world to know that Jews do have guts.'"

Dean's testimony of clear premeditation punched a devastating hole in the defense contention that Ruby was in a "fugue state" at the moment he shot Oswald. Belli objected heatedly to Dean's testimony on the grounds that no foundation had been laid for it. He moved for a mistrial, which Judge Brown overruled.

What no one on the defense team yet realized was that Sergeant Dean's alleged conversation with Ruby could not have occurred as Dean testified it had. This information came to me in June 1964, three months after Ruby's conviction, from a Dallas police department source. I didn't write about it at the time because all my attention was then devoted to reporting the story of Oswald's diary. After its publication, the tight scrutiny I was getting from the FBI made it difficult to work with certain sensitive sources.

I learned that Warren Commission investigators had come to doubt Sergeant Dean's word back in April. In fact, according to my source, they confronted Dean and accused him of lying under oath.

They caught him while investigating something else entirely— the possibility that an accomplice might have helped Jack Ruby penetrate police security that morning in the City Hall basement. Federal investigators and a contingent of local cops reviewed every available image taken in the basement before and after Oswald's death—both television footage and still photos. Though they found no evidence that Ruby had a helper, they kept seeing Sergeant Dean pop up when, according to his testimony, he was upstairs in the jail, listening to Ruby claim that he planned the Oswald murder.

I felt certain the truth about Dean's testimony would be a strong point for Ruby's appeals team, and I felt obligated to get it to them in some fashion. So I went to Phil Burleson, then a young former prosecutor who'd handled much of the organizational work for Belli in the original trial. With my source's permission, I told Phil what I knew and how I knew it—as well as who else knew it, including Henry Wade, Jim Bowie, and possibly Bill Alexander.

At some point, Phil Burleson told the Ruby family that he received the original tip about Sergeant Dean from me. Both Ruby sisters, Eileen Kaminsky in Chicago and Eva Grant in Dallas, telephoned me to express their appreciation. From that moment on, I was well connected inside the Ruby camp, especially through Eva.

⁘

Jack Ruby was never emotionally stable, not in my opinion anyway, but the assassination and Oswald's murder seemed to further destabilize him. Dr. Robert Beavers, then director of the psychiatric hospital at Southwestern Medical School, was asked by one of Ruby's lawyers, Clayton "Red" Fowler, and the court to evaluate the convicted killer mentally in the summer and fall of 1964. Ruby had been acting strangely, talking of suicide and hearing voices.

Beavers spent numerous lengthy sessions with Ruby over the next six months. He said he found the strip joint owner "bedeviled by demons—a very unstable, tormented person. Basically I had thought it was a farce, an embarrassing farce, the whole psychiatric bullshit during the trial," said Dr. Beavers. "I felt that here was a sick guy in jail, and I thought it was a way of making a statement that psychiatrists are doctors, and they see people just like in the case

154

of a person who had broken his leg; an orthopedist would go do something to help the person in jail."

Prevented because of regulations from moving Ruby to a psychiatric ward where he belonged, Beavers said he found the only way to try to help his new patient was to visit him in his jail cell regularly—which he did. "When I saw him, he was psychotic, there's no doubt about that. He'd be flipping off alternately claiming, 'I'm hearing the Jews being killed in the street,' to 'It's all my fault' and like that," recalled Beavers. "Then he would discuss something rational, normal."

I asked Beavers if Ruby seemed aware that many Americans thought he did what he did as part of a conspiracy.

"You got to remember," the psychiatrist replied, "this guy really was crazy. The outside world doesn't become that significant when you're in a six-by-nine cell and you can hear only noises—and you're crazy to boot." Dr. Beavers said in his opinion Ruby wasn't psychotic on November 24, 1963. "That's why I was embarrassed as a psychiatrist with all that nonsense, that psychomotor epilepsy defense. To my mind, that was an attorney-developed concept."

Beavers said his diagnosis was admittedly "a little shaky" because he had not seen Ruby immediately after the murder. But, he added, "You don't get rid of psychomotor epilepsy, and in my opinion, he had no evidence of it at the time I was interviewing him. He thought he was going to be a hero. That's what he talked about when he flipped to the sanity. He thought everybody would think he was great."

Ruby was kept in the Dallas county lockup pending his appeal. He telephoned his sister Eva almost every night. As the months passed, his end of the conversations grew stranger and stranger, less coherent, and apparently quite wild. Eva told me her brother ranted that all the Jews in America were being killed and that she and others were in particular danger. Somewhere he got the idea that his brother Earl had lost both his legs. Once he screamed and said he could hear "them coming for me now!"

During one of our discussions, Eva suggested I listen to Jack for myself. "Why don't you come over tonight and you can hear," she said.

What a great opportunity, I thought.

I arrived at her apartment, and soon the phone rang. It was Jack.

"How are you feeling?" Eva gushed. "Did you get what Hyman sent you? Are you sleeping better?"

After a moment, she placed her hand over the receiver, looked at me, and rolled her eyes. Jack was off on some tirade.

"Jack . . . Jack . . . Jack!" she said into the phone, trying to get his attention. "Hugh Aynesworth is here. You remember him. Ask him what you just asked me. He is a reporter. He will be truthful with you."

"Hi, Jack," I began. "How are you?"

Silence.

"Hey, I talked to a good friend of yours today."

Still nothing.

"Yeah, George Senator called me. Said he was going to try to get in to see you."

As if I'd said nothing about his old pal—who'd called to ask me if I knew anyone who'd like to buy Jack's suits—Ruby suddenly spoke up, heading off in several directions at once.

"I've got this bad headache, never stops," he said. "You'd think they'd give me something for it. But they won't. They want me to suffer."

Pause.

"This place stinks. You come down and see. Bill Decker will let you in."

I tried with no luck to pose a couple of questions, and Ruby gave me no indication that he even knew with whom he was speaking. He complained about the medicines he was receiving and said he had stomach pains.

"Are you Jewish?"

"No, I'm not."

"Well, you wouldn't understand what we are going through, then. Do you know I'm the only Jew in this jail?"

I doubted that and was pondering my reply when Eva motioned for me to return the receiver to her. "They allow only so much time," she explained.

After she hung up, we spoke for a few minutes. Eva promised I could return later in the week. But when I called her, she was ill. Other matters intruded, and I didn't see her again until Jack's death.

That was quite an occasion.

In late December 1966, Jack Ruby lay in Parkland Hospital in Dallas, dying of stomach cancer in the same facility where President Kennedy and Oswald had expired. At the time, I was briefly out of journalism, working as the public relations director for the George A. Fuller Company, a major international builder. The job had been interesting and far better paying than journalism, yet I missed the news business. After a few months among the suits, I had just agreed to go to work for *Newsweek* in its Houston bureau.

On January 3, 1967, as I was having a cup of coffee in a cafeteria along Interstate 35, just northwest of downtown Dallas, I heard the report on a local radio news program: "Jack Ruby is dead. Authorities at Parkland Hospital announced that the former nightclub owner died of cancer this morning."

Officially, I was still a PR man. The *Newsweek* gig wasn't to start for three weeks. I called New York anyway and spoke to the magazine's chief of correspondents, Rod Gander.

"Do you want me to handle it?" I asked a little breathlessly.

"Yes, of course," Gander told me.

A journalist once more, I drove like crazy to Parkland. As I pulled up to the front entrance, Earl Ruby, together with sisters Eva and Eileen, hustled out the door.

"Come with us!" Earl said, taking my arm. "I'll bring you back later."

"Yes! Yes! Hugh can help us," said Mrs. Kaminsky.

I had no idea how that might be so but was more than happy to accompany them. Earl drove us to the Weiland-Merritt funeral home just east of downtown on Live Oak Street. Two newspaper photographers were right behind us.

On the way, Eva began to sob. "Jack's gone! Jack's gone!" She wiped her tears with a multicolored handkerchief. Of them all, Eva was closest to Jack. She often helped him manage his Dallas clubs and frequently offered business advice, which he followed. "He didn't act like he knew he was dying," she said. "He called me a couple of nights ago, and we had the best talk."

"But he still believed in this conspiracy stuff, didn't he?" asked Eileen. "Last time I talked to Jack he told me that unless I could pretend I wasn't Jewish, I'd be killed. I told him I didn't know how to do that."

When we got to the funeral home, Earl pulled around back, and the four of us hurried into a bare anteroom. A small herd of reporters and photographers quickly gathered outside, most of them my close acquaintants, some of them pounding on the doors. One photographer scrambled up the side of the building to reach a ledge from where he could shoot pictures down into the room. I hoped no one would suggest that I go outside to join my unruly friends.

Earl and Eva broke into an argument over whether or not their dead brother, an army veteran, qualified for a government-paid funeral. Eileen excused herself and headed for a telephone. "Have to alert so many people in Chicago," she said.

The funeral home director, trying to keep the group calm, assured Earl and Eva that he could check out any possible benefit. He sat them down and asked to which Chicago funeral home Mr. Ruby's body was to be sent.

"Old Original Weinstein & Sons," said Earl. "We go back a long way with them."

"Okay. Let's start with his birth date."

That was a problem. None of the three siblings knew the date. All three guessed different days.

"It was March 25, 1911," I said, speaking up for the first time. In fact, according to the Warren Commission report, nobody knows precisely what day Jacob Rubenstein was born in Chicago. March 25, 1911, was the date Ruby himself most often gave.

Then Earl and the funeral executive began to discuss the costs of preparing and shipping his brother home for burial. The price of the casket nearly choked poor Earl, who had good reason to wish that costs were kept down. I know he had spent $100,000 or so of his own money on Jack's legal defense, and Earl was not a rich man.

Unlike Lee Harvey Oswald's wife and mother, the Ruby clan was no good at making crime pay. One sorry attempt I know of involved smuggling a tape machine into Jack's hospital room to capture his voice for a phonograph record they hoped to sell in cahoots with some operator from California. They got the recorder into the room all right but made the mistake of resting the machine on a radiator. The record that was ultimately produced and sold in small quantities that quickly vanished included the radiator's full metallic repertoire in the background, from steamy hisses to angry bangs.

"But you will want a nice casket," the funeral man pressed on. He said he could offer Earl a good deal. That's when a thought occurred to me. I'd read somewhere that some states required burial in a locally sold casket when a body is shipped in from out of state. So I motioned to Earl that I'd like a private word with him and shared what I knew.

Maybe all they needed to get Jack to Chicago was a simple pine box.

"Oh yes! I was going to mention that to you, Mr. Ruby," the annoyed funeral man said. "No need buying an expensive casket here in Texas."

Business finished, we made our escape out the back.

On the way to my car, Earl turned and said, "Hugh, you're going to be with us, aren't you?"

I said I'd have to check with *Newsweek*.

"My God, yes," Rod Gander said over the phone. "Call when you hit the ground."

Phil Burleson, another invitee, and I checked into a motel close to the Weinstein funeral home in Chicago and took a cab together to Eileen's house. We'd been asked to join the family the night before the funeral. I was a bit apprehensive since I'd never been inside a Jewish temple, much less attended a Jewish funeral.

As we were instructed, Phil and I washed our hands in a pan just outside the door, then walked inside Eileen's modest south-side residence. The interior was sparsely furnished. Pictures were turned to the wall. People sat quietly on benches and crates. Some prayed. I was self-conscious, worried about displacing my yarmulke, the Jewish skullcap.

Oddly, earlier in the day, a Catholic nun appeared at Weinstein's and requested to see the body. When refused, she left without signing the register. Three priests came the night before with the same request—when cordially denied, they knelt in the snow outside, briefly prayed, and departed.

Later that evening, a problem arose. One of Ruby's pallbearers became ill and could not make the service the next day. A cousin suggested they contact one of Jack's boyhood friends, now in the upholstery business. But then someone else informed the group that Sid, the upholsterer, had been dead for five years.

Earl took me aside. "Could you do it?" he asked quietly.

I was torn. The Rubys were a decent family, compassionate and loving. They did not deserve the pain that Jack caused them. What Earl asked was a simple favor that I'd be happy to do under any other circumstances. However, it seemed hypocritical if I, who genuinely disliked Jack Ruby, helped carry him to his grave.

"I don't think I'm the proper man," I told Earl.

"Why not?"

"Because while I like all of you, I did not like Jack, and I knew him pretty well. Any person has the right to have those who loved and respected him carry him those last few yards."

Luckily, Eileen and Eva soon found an old schoolmate to fill in. "Damn, Hugh, why did you turn 'em down?" asked Burleson, who would be one of the pallbearers, as we rode back to the motel that night. "I thought Eileen was going to cry."

I think I told Phil that *Newsweek* might frown on a correspondent's becoming part of a story he covered, which I guess was probably true, but it wasn't the reason I refused. It was my call, and I didn't think I should do it.

The next morning was cold and snowy. Scores of reporters showed up to cover the funeral but were kept behind police barricades. I was the only member of the press allowed inside the sanctuary, where a brief service was held.

Before the rites, I voiced a concern to Earl and his brother Hyman. With all the conspiracy talk already around, I worried that someday someone would say that the man in Jack Ruby's grave was not Jack Ruby.

This was not an idle fear. A British barrister named Michael Eddowes later argued in a book that Lee Harvey Oswald was not buried in his grave. Some Russian spy supposedly was moldering there. Eddowes agitated to have Oswald exhumed. Robert Oswald was horrified by the idea. Marina, after the application of a certain amount of cash, approved the deal.

In 1981, her dead husband was dug up. A team of scientists led by Dallas forensic pathologist Linda Norton examined the remains, declared they were Oswald's, and the assassin was reinterred with a casket upgrade. The old one apparently leaked.

My proposal to the Ruby family was to allow a pool of reporters into the sanctuary just before they closed Jack's casket for the last time, in order to attest that Jack Ruby actually was in it. That way no one, ever, could concoct some phony excuse for disinterring Ruby.

"That would be so horrible," said Eileen.

"OK, we'll do it," Earl said. "I'll work it out some way." He conferred with a lawyer friend, Alan Adelson, who agreed it was a sound idea.

So for a couple of minutes, three Chicago reporters came into the cemetery sanctuary, viewed Jack Ruby in his casket, and left. The only one of the three I now remember was Nelson Benton of CBS.

Eva and I stayed in touch for a while until she decided to move to California and live with her son. Just before she left, she called me to say she wanted to give me something "for being so kind to the Ruby family."

She had two of Jack's neckties, "and I want you to have them." It was a touching gesture, which I deeply appreciated and said so. I told Eva that I'd stop by her apartment for them soon.

I never did.

CHAPTER THIRTEEN

Bob Schieffer's Coup

Reporters tackle national tragedies such as the Kennedy assassination with much the same verve as firefighters rush to an eight-alarm blaze. The pressure is often immense. Sometimes the memories hang around for a long, long time. You wouldn't want to do it every day.

"It took me a long time to get over the assassination," CBS newsman Bob Schieffer told me. "I was so emotionally spent. Not until 9/11 did I again have that same kind of feeling as I covered a story."

Of all the reportorial skills that come into play when covering a major catastrophe, the abilities to think quickly, act on instinct, and improvise are among the most important. Bob, then a reporter for the *Star-Telegram*, was handling the rewrite desk telephones on the afternoon of November 22 when a woman called to ask if anyone at the paper could give her a ride to Dallas.

"Lady," Schieffer told her, "you know the president has just been shot, and besides, we're not a taxi service."

"Yes, I heard it on the radio," she replied. "I think the person they've arrested is my son."

Schieffer told Marguerite Oswald to sit tight; he'd be right over. But first he needed appropriate wheels. "I had this little Triumph TR4 sports car then," he said. "I didn't want to drive her over in that." So he asked the paper's automotive editor, Bill Foster, what kind of car he was reviewing that week. When Foster said he was driving a Cadillac, Schieffer decided that the two of them would chauffeur Mrs. Oswald to Dallas.

Schieffer made sure the *Star-Telegram* received full value for the favor. On the way to Dallas, he conducted the first interview with the accused assassin's mother. Then he used her to penetrate the inner offices of the Dallas police department. "I just walked up to the first uniformed Dallas policeman that I saw," he recalled, "and said, 'I'm the one who brought Oswald's mother over. Is there any place we can put her so these reporters won't talk to her?'"

The officer found a cubby hole in the Burglary and Theft Bureau where Schieffer stashed Marguerite and then surreptitiously passed back and forth into the hallway, gathering up *Star-Telegram* reporters' notes, which he then phoned back to the city desk from his hideaway.

Mrs. Oswald had astounded Schieffer with her conversation on the drive from Fort Worth. "It was a great lesson for me," he explained, "because she said such outrageous things. She was already talking about how the wife would get all the money and people would feel sorry for her. Marguerite was the mother and she would be forgotten.

"I just thought, this poor woman is under such strain and such pressure that she can't mean what she's saying. Some of the stuff I didn't put into the Saturday paper. Well it turned out that she was obsessed with money. It was all she had on her mind. Even years later, she'd call me at CBS and say, 'Is there any way CBS would pay me for an interview?' Oh, she was awful. She really was a villain."

Sunday afternoon, Schieffer was part of another *Star-Telegram* coup. Over at the *News*, Jack Beers had just developed his extraordinary photo of Ruby about to shoot Oswald in the City Hall basement. Standing next to him in the darkroom was Bob Jarboe, the AP photographer, who doubled as a wire photo operator. "Beers seemed transfixed by the image," Jarboe recalled. "He just sort of fell back against the wall and told me to make two prints for him." Jarboe also made two prints for the AP, which sent the stunning photo out over its wires within the hour.

A short while later, Bill Rives, assistant managing editor at the *News*, approached Jarboe with a smug expression. "We've got a picture I bet you'd love to have," Rives smiled.

"You mean this one?" Jarboe replied, holding up a copy of the Beers photo.

"Rives went bananas," Jarboe remembers.

When the Beers picture popped up on the AP machine over at the *Star-Telegram* that Sunday afternoon, managing editor Loren McMullin decided to use the photo to anchor a special Sunday afternoon edition, essentially scooping the *News* with its own picture.

"We were just thrilled to death," said Schieffer, who phoned in copy from Dallas to the newsroom in Fort Worth for the special edition. "We all just worked our asses off. Everybody had no sleep. We were all worn out. But man, when that *Star-Telegram* truck came by, I just grabbed a bundle of those papers and took 'em right down there to Dealey Plaza. I don't think journalism is like that anymore."

Eddie Barker, news director at KRLD-TV, gambled big time and came up a winner. Broadcasting from the Dallas Trade Mart on Friday, Eddie got a tip from a doctor at Parkland that Kennedy was dead a few minutes before the official announcement. While the competition over at WFAA-TV was forced to wait for confirmation, Eddie broadcast what he had.

"When I announced this over the air," he told me, "the network panicked. The validity of my source was questioned. However I knew this man was trustworthy, so I kept repeating that the president was dead."

In a later *Journalism Quarterly* article, Richard K. Van der Karr called Barker's announcement one of the most important events of the weekend. "It will certainly be one of the greatest snap evaluations of a source in the history of broadcast journalism," wrote Van der Karr.

Bert Shipp, assistant news director at WFAA-TV, got the same tip about the same time—from Bill Decker, a man all the media trusted. The sheriff had told Shipp there was no way the president could be alive, that the entire back of his head had been blown off. Shipp told his bosses, vouched for the source, and begged them to broadcast it. But he was told the news director had provided a recent directive: "No more dead people mentioned without death certificates."

Associated Press reporter Mike Cochran's long weekend started Thursday night in Fort Worth, where he helped host White House staffers, the press corps, and assorted federal agents at the Fort Worth Press Club bar. They partied until three in the morning, when Cochran went home. However, some Secret Service agents and reporters weren't quite ready to stop. Several of them went on to The Cellar, a late-late place. Disclosure of this revelry got the group in serious trouble after the assassination next day.

Friday morning, Cochran was at Carswell Air Force Base to make sure Air Force One lifted off on time with the president inside. He filed what was called a floating bulletin, a brief advisory to editors that "President Kennedy left Carswell at 10:45 this morning." Driving back from the military base, Cochran and his wife, Sondra, were caught in a hopeless traffic jam. So they went to breakfast, and she dropped him off at the AP office in the *Star-Telegram* building.

Minutes later Cochran heard a copy boy screaming, "The president's been shot!" as he ripped the AP bulletin from the wire machine. Cochran tried to reach Dallas by telephone, but the lines were jammed. So he teamed up with *Star-Telegram* reporter Jack

Tinsley and other staffers, and they raced to Parkland Hospital in Tinsley's car.

"We got within two blocks," Cochran recalled, "and couldn't get any closer. Tinsley just abandoned his car in the middle of the street, and we ran on up. When we walked in the front door, here came a wave of nurses. My memory of this is so vivid. Three or four nurses were just sobbing, almost hysterical. You don't often see nurses get that emotional. I said, 'Kennedy's dead.' We learned later that Malcolm Kilduff had just announced it."

Cochran stayed at Parkland long enough to file an update on Governor Connally's condition, then headed for the AP's Dallas office, where he worked through the night. Sunday morning, he drove home to Fort Worth to shower and change his clothes. He expected to head back to Dallas where he was to relieve fellow reporter Peggy Simpson on the AP's Oswald watch at City Hall. Sondra greeted him at the door with news that Oswald had been shot, so Cochran hurried back to the Dallas office to man the desk.

"We started getting telephone calls from papers, wanting a story on Jack Beers' 'Pulitzer' photograph," said Cochran. "I hadn't seen it. Then Bob Johnson, the Dallas bureau chief asked, 'Can't we do a story on this thing?' We were just besieged by calls. A couple of hours later, people started asking about Bob Jackson's 'Pulitzer' picture. I wrote a piece about the two without ever having seen them. I really can't remember what I said. Of course, I can't remember a lot about that weekend."

Then came one of the rare embarrassments of Cochran's long and distinguished career. Though only two years out of college and fairly new to the AP, he was nonetheless assigned to write the overnight story on Oswald. This was a very big deal, one of perhaps five or six major stories the wire service would promote to its member news organizations around the world. "I cleverly wrote a lead that, in effect, convicted Lee Harvey Oswald," Cochran explained, "saying he'd probably go down as the most hated person in American history, or something like that. Somehow it got past the Dallas editors, and

New York had to file a 'bulletin kill' on my lead. A bulletin kill was the most disgraceful thing you could have happen to you. Raping the president's daughter didn't even compare."

There were a number of far more doubtful stories that eluded an editor's vigilance that day. Some of these errors could be attributed to the stress, confusion, and turmoil of the weekend. But some articles were just plain schlock to start with—imaginative reporting.

Seth Kantor, a former *Times Herald* reporter who was covering JFK's Texas visit for the Scripps-Howard newspapers, wrote "sometime between 1:30 and 2 p.m." on Friday, Jack Ruby stopped and spoke to him inside the main entrance to Parkland Hospital. Tugging at Kantor's clothing, the reporter claimed, Ruby asked, "Should I close my places for the next three nights, do you think?"

A good tale, but probably untrue. Ruby denied ever going to the hospital that day, and the Warren Commission concluded that Kantor was mistaken, that Ruby's whereabouts were well documented, except for about a twenty-minute period that afternoon, certainly not enough time for Ruby to have driven his car through the melee toward Parkland and then returned to downtown Dallas.

In a story filed after Ruby killed Oswald, Kantor typed a stirring lead: "Dallas—In disbelief, I watched a friend of mine, Jack Ruby, gun to death the man charged with killing President Kennedy."

Kantor continued: "It happened less than ten feet from where I was standing in the basement of the Dallas police station. The last time I had seen Oswald's killer, Ruby, was two days earlier. It was at Parkland Memorial Hospital, moments before the news was official that President Kennedy was dead."

Kantor, whose former *Times Herald* pals laughed at his claim that Ruby had been a friend, later published a conspiracy theory book, *The Ruby Cover-Up*. In it he concocted a tale that somebody phoned Ruby Sunday morning and instructed him to kill Oswald. "A call was placed to the unlisted phone number in Ruby's apartment; Ruby was told where to enter the station and that the transfer van was en route. Ruby made sure the snub-nosed gun with its two-inch barrel was loaded. He put it in his trouser pocket. Never in his jacket. It got the jacket out of shape."

Another faker was Thayer Waldo at the *Star-Telegram*. In February 1964, Waldo wrote that the government was holding in protective custody a close eyewitness who could solidly identify Oswald as Kennedy's assassin. When this so-called exclusive ran in the paper's early editions, the Associated Press called me for comment. I said there was a solid witness, but that as far as I knew he wasn't being held anywhere.

This wasn't the first factual leap I'd seen Waldo take. I think I termed it "a bunch of crap." Justice Department spokesman Edwin O. Guthman concurred. "There is no truth to the story at all," said Guthman, "and no such witness exists."

"The story," Mike Cochran remembered, "was a front-page banner to start with. After the AP talked to you, it became about two paragraphs on the last page of the paper. Oh, you talk about an embarrassing cover-up! Thayer Waldo was awful. He became a laughingstock."

Richard Dudman in the *St. Louis Post-Dispatch* also had a great story. He wrote that Kennedy could not have been shot from behind because Dudman had seen entry bullet holes in the limousine's windshield. Alas that scoop went up in smoke when authorities allowed reporters to examine the hole-free windshield, which was nicked from the inside.

While the print outlets, who broke most of the important stories, bungled a few, the electronic media also made missteps. CBS, best remembered for Walter Cronkite's emotional announcement of Kennedy's death, ran a dubious story about alleged FBI advance knowledge of JFK's assassination—a tale that did not withstand critical inquiry but enjoyed wide approval among conspiracy buffs.

William B. Walter, a clerk who had worked out of the FBI's New Orleans office in 1963, told conspiracy monger Mark Lane in 1968 that FBI headquarters sent a telex bulletin to all its domestic offices on November 17, 1963, warning that there might be an assassination attempt in Dallas and alerting its agents to check closely with their informants.

Walter said he was the only one who saw the memo that night— although four others later saw the teletype. This is what he claimed to have seen:

URGENT TO ALL SACS FROM DIRECTOR

Threat to assassinate President Kennedy in Dallas, Texas, November 22-23. Information received by the Bureau has determined that a militant revolutionary group may attempt to assassinate President Kennedy on his proposed trip to Dallas, Texas.

Walter said he contacted several superiors in the bureau and was told never to mention the teletype. Nevertheless he claimed he kept a copy and locked the original in a bank vault.

At the time, Lane, or somebody close to New Orleans DA Jim Garrison, mentioned Walter to Martin "Moe" Waldron of the *New York Times*. Waldron then mentioned Walter to Jerry Cohen of the *Los Angeles Times* and me over dinner one night. We all had a laugh over it. "There is bizarre and there is bizarre," Waldron said as he explained what Walter was peddling.

We didn't expect to hear of it again, but often those who make up such stories, no matter how unbelievable, don't just chuck them. Frequently it's all that makes them feel important, as though they are *somebody*. Consequently they are prone to recycling their tales.

In this case, Lane passed Walter's assertions along to Garrison, who was conducting a high-profile, low-road investigation of the assassination. Garrison was also battling with NBC News at the time. The DA had threatened to sue the network after a June 1967 NBC *White Paper* documentary showed his investigation to be a sham as I had written in a *Newsweek* article the month before.

Anyway, NBC late-night host Johnny Carson invited Garrison to spend a full hour on his program January 31, 1968. Carson allowed the DA to malign his detractors and generally argue his alleged case against businessman Clay Shaw, whom he accused of conspiring to kill the president. During the show, Garrison also tossed out the name of William Walter and dignified his fantasy tale by repeating it before a national television audience.

The FBI quickly investigated, interviewing more than fifty agents and supervisors, checking messaging in and out, even contacting several offices. Officials decided that Walter, who had left the FBI after being placed on probation, was lying.

Most everybody forgot about William Walter until 1975 when my partner at the *Times Herald*, Bob Dudney, learned the onetime clerk was spreading his FBI bulletin story once again. Dudney and I interviewed Walter for the paper. When I heard his story, I didn't believe it. But we had to nail it down. So we took copious notes and then flew Walter to Dallas for a polygraph test.

We also called a number of individuals whom Walter claimed knew something of the memo or could vouch for his veracity. We even secured a complete list of FBI telexes for several of the days surrounding the date of the alleged bulletin. Each was in numerical order, and there was no memo to the SACs such as Walter had described among them.

He started changing his story. First he said he had been an agent, but he wasn't—just a clerk. Another time he gave us a list of those he contacted in the hours immediately following the arrival of the alleged telex. That list changed as several people denied talking to him. Then he said he didn't have his handwritten copy of the telex anymore because he had given it to CBS News, where it apparently had vanished.

Walter seemed confident, energetic, a pleasant fellow. Bill Burnham, the well-qualified polygraph operator we used at the paper on several important sources in the 1970s, said he didn't believe him. Yet officially, Burnham called the test "inconclusive."

Almost everything Walter told us changed once we contacted any of his witnesses or associates. We fully realized the importance of the story, if true, and also knew how unfair and harmful it would be if untrue. So *Times Herald* editors, with Dudney and me in complete agreement, concluded it should not be printed.

Meantime we learned that CBS might be going ahead with its own story, based on Walter's fabrications. Our publisher, Tom Johnson, was a personal friend of Dan Rather and felt he should warn Rather away from the story, believing that we had spent more time investigating it than CBS had. Johnson wanted to give Rather knowledgeable input.

They talked, and Rather called back a couple of times as a follow-up. Both Dudney and I told him what we knew and that we felt there was nothing to Walter's story. We expected CBS to kill the piece. Instead they ran it aggressively. We responded the next day with an extensive front-page knock-down story, outlining the holes and misstatements in the account Walter gave to the network.

In 1978, after the House Subcommittee on Assassinations interviewed Walter, they also concluded he manufactured the story. Walter was still having trouble finding anyone to corroborate his version of events. He told the committee his former wife, Sharon Covert, who had also worked for the FBI in New Orleans, might be able to back him up. But Covert advised the committee that she could not support any of his allegations. Moreover Walter had never mentioned any such bureau communication to her during their marriage.

Still later, when the JFK Assassinations Records Review Board convened in 1996, Marina Oswald—by then a self-described conspiracy theorist—wrote its chairman John Tunheim asking what the board was doing about releasing "the full particulars and original of the teletype received by Mr. Walter."

She had read about it in a recent book, Marina said, adding, "I now believe that my former husband met with the Dallas FBI on November 16, 1963, and provided informant information on which this teletype was based."

A story like Walter's, legitimized by a respected media outfit, can live on forever, no matter how slim its proof or believability.

One of the more absurd tales—quite literally far out—was cooked up by former *Star-Telegram* reporter Jim Marrs in a book called *Alien Agenda*. Marrs, one of the best-known conspiracy buffs, became semi-famous, and somewhat more solvent, when filmmaker Oliver Stone bought his book, *Crossfire* to make his 1991 movie, *JFK*.

In the subsequent *Alien Agenda*, Marrs pondered whether Kennedy was killed because the president knew all about alien visitation to Earth and someone didn't want him to tell the American people. Among his sources was an individual named Bill Holden, whom Marrs described as "loadmaster" for Air Force One. Holden supposedly asked Kennedy what he thought of aliens having visited Earth. The president paused, according to Holden, then said, "I'd like to tell the public about the alien situation, but my hands are tied."

In Marrs' words, "spurred on by such tantalizing bits of evidence, some researchers even claimed that Kennedy's assassination was to prevent him from revealing the news of extraterrestrial visitation to the public."

I once asked the author at a university debate if he really believed such "tantalizing evidence."

"What should I have done," he replied, "ignored it?"

While the actions of Marrs and most other journalists didn't affect me personally, the egregious behavior of the legendary Bob Considine was most painful to me. Considine, then writing for the *New York Journal-American*, was a true icon of my trade.

When Considine came to Dallas to cover the Ruby trial for the paper, he contacted me. Over time, we became pretty close. We sat together in court, often ate lunch together, and frequently met for drinks with other journalists after everyone's daily stories had been filed.

One day during this period, I received yet another tip of a purported connection between Ruby and Oswald. It was a long shot, just like all the other conspiracy tips I've received. Nevertheless it was an intriguing story I felt obliged to run down.

The characters included an Oak Cliff car salesman named Warren Reynolds, who was among the witnesses who claimed to have seen Lee Harvey Oswald flee the J. D. Tippit murder scene. On the night of January 23, 1964, while closing up his brother Johnnie's used car lot on East Jefferson, Reynolds was shot one time in the head by an unknown attacker. He survived.

The next day, an anonymous caller told Johnnie Reynolds he should go see "Dago," whose real name was Darrell Wayne Garner. He was a twenty-four-year-old local ne'er-do-well familiar to the cops in connection with the attack on Warren. Johnnie notified the police, who quickly established that Garner had been at the car lot earlier in the day, and left in evident rage when Johnnie Reynolds refused to buy a 1957 Oldsmobile from him because Garner lacked a valid title for the vehicle.

Garner was arrested and released after an alibi witness, Nancy Jane Mooney, 24, said she was out drinking and driving around with him until half past three in the morning. The woman passed a polygraph test as did Garner—twice.

Then Nancy Mooney, who also went by the name of Betty MacDonald, got into a brawl with her roommate, Patsy Moore. She was arrested and jailed for disturbing the peace. Mooney aka MacDonald, who suffered from bouts of severe depression, hanged herself by her toreador slacks in her cell. In the ensuing investigation, Patsy Moore told the police that Mooney was a former stripper who'd worked at various bars in Dallas, including Jack Ruby's Carousel Club. Mooney in fact had told the police the same thing in an earlier interview.

Here's the conspiracy spin on this tawdry tale: Reynolds somehow knew too much about the Kennedy assassination and needed to be silenced. To accomplish that, Jack Ruby found a willing killer, Dago Garner, via his former employee, Mooney, whom he then had murdered in jail to cover his tracks.

The problem with this theory was none of these elements stood the test of inquiry. I found out that Mooney really did commit suicide. She'd tried it several times before and had the scars on her wrists to prove it. Despite the polygraph results, the Dallas police were convinced Dago Garner really did shoot Warren Reynolds, but his motive was anger over the Oldsmobile, not Lee Harvey Oswald.

Finally neither George Senator nor anyone else connected to the Carousel Club had any recall of Mooney working there. I also posed the question directly to Ruby, via Phil Burleson, during his trial. The lawyer reported to me that Jack knew nothing of either Mooney or Garner.

One day when I had missed a morning session of the trial, Considine asked me where I had been. I told him I had been digging on a story I thought might be really valuable but that it had turned south on me. At dinner that evening, I explained the complicated allegation but said, "It just isn't there."

"So you don't think there's anything at all to it?"

"Not unless you make up a lot of it."

Later in the week, an AP photographer called me, wondering if I could help him find photos of Garner and Warren Reynolds.

"What for?"

"Oh," he said, "the *Journal-American* in New York wants their pictures for some feature story they're working on."

Sure enough, on Sunday, February 23, Considine published "Violent Dallas: A New Chapter," telling his readers that the major suspect in the Reynolds shooting had been freed from jail on the say-so of one of Jack Ruby's strippers, who then killed herself.

When I asked Considine why he'd printed a story he knew to be false, he shrugged, "Oh, it's just a yarn."

Of course it was, until a journalist of Considine's considerable credibility and clout legitimized it in print. General Walker saw the story and invited Reynolds to come visit him. Together Walker and Reynolds decided the shooting had to be connected to Oswald. The general later telegraphed the Warren Commission, wondering why Reynolds had not been called as a witness. Still later, Jim Garrison would rehash the story as part of the conspiracy carnival he was gearing up in New Orleans.

Dago Garner eventually claimed that there really was a conspiracy involved.

＊＊＊

It was in some ways easier to publish such a "yarn" back in Considine's day, a fact with which TV talk show host Bill O'Reilly became acquainted in early 2013.

The year before, O'Reilly and co-author Martin Dugard issued their best-selling *Killing Kennedy: The End of Camelot* in which O'Reilly claims that on March 29, 1977, then a young reporter for WFAA in Dallas, he traveled to Florida to interview George de Mohrenschildt, a Russian émigré and friend of Lee Harvey Oswald whom some conspiracy buffs believe was a CIA agent.

De Mohrenschildt shot himself to death on the day in question. O'Reilly recalls in *Killing Kennedy* that he was standing on de Mohrenshildt's doorstep when he heard "the shotgun blast that marked the suicide."

That's a "fib," reported journalist Jefferson Morley in February, 2013, on the website, *JFK Facts*, which he moderates. Morley tracked down taped telephone conversations that prove O'Reilly's tale is "mostly imaginary," as Morley put it. "In fact, a reporter named Bill O'Reilly was in Dallas, Texas, on that day."

CHAPTER FOURTEEN

A Lot of Money—Almost

I think of Rodney Stalls as a pioneer, an original. On his own, the unemployed engineer developed a conspiracy theory within hours of JFK's assassination and presented it to me—his second choice—along with his so-called proof by that night.

Mr. Stalls was only the first.

One Saturday morning shortly after the assassination as I sat at my front row desk in the newsroom, a tall, painfully thin man who stank something awful came up to me. It was not at all unusual for the public to wander around the newsroom in those days. It was a much simpler time.

"I'm from the Windy City," he said, "and I've got the story for you. I know how Oswald got the message. They got to me too."

I placed him in a chair and rolled my own back a distance to get away from the stench. He leaned down and rubbed his leg, then stood up painfully and lifted his trouser leg to reveal a horrendous abscess, red and gray and oozing pus.

"That's how my leg got torn up," he said.

It was necessary to think very quickly.

"Stop right there," I said. "I'm just a lowly reporter. I don't feel capable of handling what you have to share. So let me give you someone who handles sensitive issues for us. And one other thing, don't tell him you talked to me first because he might get angry."

Then I pointed my visitor toward Assistant Managing Editor Bill Rives, one of the nicer people at the paper, upon whom the rest of us were always playing practical jokes. Rives, who spoke to the man from Chicago for two hours that morning, never learned that I had sent him in.

My colleague Larry Grove once jokingly threatened to blackmail me.

Tom Simmons, the other assistant managing editor who shared an office with Rives, later mentioned they had to burn candles for days to get rid of the smell after the Chicago man left.

Still another early conspiracy buff was a local attorney, Carroll Jarnagin. He made a provocative claim to have overheard Lee Harvey Oswald in deep conversation at the Carousel Club with Jack Ruby a few days before November 22.

Jarnagin, who looked to be about forty-five years old, had the tired face of a drinker. He was evasive throughout our conversation—he did offer me snippets of direct dialogue, but these later changed. He avoided eye contact and frequently scratched himself. But the major problem with his assertion was that he had no proof. He did have a girlfriend who substantiated Jarnagin's claim to have visited the Carousel Club one night in early November, but she remembered nothing about the alleged Oswald-Ruby chat.

When the lawyer later took his story to Chief Curry and Henry Wade, they gave him a polygraph test, which he failed. "He grinned and said, 'Well, some things you remember and others you don't,' and walked out. I never heard of him again," said DA Wade.

Yet—and this part of Jarnagin's story amazed me—the Warren Commission dithered over a version of this yarn for months.

Jarnagin's name was never mentioned, but in March 1964, Mark Lane, the author of *Rush to Judgment* published in 1966, testified that he had a source who had overheard a lengthy plot session in the Carousel Club.

The kooks and opportunists kept coming, with theories and stories in every imaginable flavor. Some, like Mr. Stalls or "Stinky" from Chicago, popped up out of nowhere. Others I thought of as my regulars. This group—which included one woman—wrote, called, or showed up in person as often as weekly, always willing to share some new tidbit, some new twist.

In the early days, their paranoia centered mostly on the Russians or H. L. Hunt or General Walker, singly or in combination. Occasionally a buff would bring up the Bay of Pigs and link Kennedy's mishandling of the 1961 Cuban invasion debacle to his 1963 assassination.

J. Edgar Hoover was another early conspiracy favorite. Most of the alleged plots involving the FBI director began with the assumption that JFK planned to replace the old despot if reelected in 1964. The recurring rumors, stoked by Lonnie Hudkin's unfortunate article that Lee Harvey Oswald was a paid federal informant, lent credence to these stories.

<hr />

The *News* jumped my salary in December 1963 to $9,500 a year, thanks to being in the right places at the right times in late November. It had not occurred to me that I might exploit my situation for a whole lot more money, not until I got the call from New York.

Two people were on the other end of the line—a Frenchman I'll call François, and Doris, an American book agent. "Everyone in Europe agrees with you about the Kennedy assassination," François began in heavily accented English. "And I am a well-known literary publisher who wants to get to the bottom of this. You know, our people loved Mr. Kennedy."

I had no clue what part of my thinking had registered so positively with the collective French psyche. As I spoke with François and Doris, I thought back to a recent panel discussion in New York I'd participated in. The wire services quoted me saying there were still too many unanswered questions in the case. I figured that was where François was coming from, and he admitted later that, yes, this was how he discovered me.

His proposal was simple and left me a bit breathless. François offered me $75,000 to produce, within three months, a book of fifty to sixty thousand words that addressed what he called "problems" with the evidence against Oswald: the "probability" that Oswald had once been a U.S. agent of some sort and that the newly formed Warren Commission would be politically tainted, nothing more than a tool for President Johnson.

"With your reputation and the fact that you were there," François said, "this will be a very important book. It will sweep Europe." I told him I'd have to think it over and that I needed some time. He agreed.

The offer stunned me. To date, besides my regular stringing income from *Newsweek* and my recent $500 raise at the *News*, the only extra money I'd seen was the twenty-five dollars that the Newspaper Enterprise Association paid me to recap the first weekend of the story.

I decided to seek Larry Grove's advice. Larry grinned when I told him about the $75,000. "You'd better get an agent and a good one," he said. Then he told me about a deal he once thought he had to write a small book about his World War II adventures in the South Pacific. "It started at $10,000. Then the guy called and said he had to make a special distribution deal and therefore could pay me only $8,000. Then he tried to get it even cheaper than that. He kept saying, 'You don't need an agent. It'll cost you most of what you make. Stick with me.' In the end, I got to thinking my deal wasn't so good and I'd end up paying him, so I just eased out of it."

As we spoke and Grove considered my situation, he observed that the Frenchman clearly wanted a conspiracy book, and one written by the newsman with the deepest personal knowledge of the assassination probably could be a best seller. "But don't ruin your reputation for a few fast bucks," he warned.

That remark made us both laugh. A few fast bucks? How about the near equivalent of both our salaries for almost five years!

François called the next day to discuss the book again. The more we spoke the less I liked the idea and the less I liked François. He was very full of himself, very pushy. At last I told him someone was at the door and got off the phone. As he rang off, he told me to expect a call from Doris, the agent. Doris and I spoke several times before I finally said I couldn't do the project because the *News* wouldn't let me.

"But you don't make that kind of money at the newspaper," she argued with a decided Brooklyn accent.

"Yes, but they don't tell me what to write, either," I replied.

And that was that.

When I later told my managing editor, Jack Krueger, about the failed negotiations, he slapped me on the back, said "Good choice, Hugh," and a month later raised my pay another ten dollars a week.

When I recounted the episode to my wife, she was none too pleased. "Do you realize how much money that was?" she asked, incredulous. I replied with that old line from my home state, West Virginia, about how you can put lipstick on a sow but that won't make her homecoming queen.

My wife wasn't amused. Never would be.

CHAPTER FIFTEEN

Lane and Garrison: Two of a Kind

In my view, were it not for the pervasive influence of a handful of individuals, there would be no plague of conspiracy theories surrounding the Kennedy assassination.

The first of these regrettable characters was Lee Harvey Oswald himself, an inadequate mope who seemed to many people incapable of pulling off such a heinous and spectacular crime on his own. Reason seemed to dictate that he must have had help, that he really was a patsy, someone's tool.

Second was Jack Ruby. By usurping the executioner's role, the emotionally unstable strip club owner created generations of doubters and not unreasonably so. It was an audacious, desperate act that would seem to make sense only if Jack Ruby had a very powerful, rational motive for killing Lee Harvey Oswald.

But he didn't.

Ruby did not know Oswald, had never seen, spoken, or written to him, nor did the two men share any other known connection, sinister or otherwise. They were total strangers in every sense of the word. The hard evidence in the case supports no other conclusion. Based on indisputable facts, I believe that Ruby acted spontaneously in the basement of City Hall. The opportunity to kill the presidential assassin suddenly presented itself, and Ruby acted accordingly. But for sheer coincidence, he might just as well have been driving home from the Western Union office at that moment.

The third of these key actors was Mark Lane, for whose excesses I must shoulder some blame. I foolishly gave Lane a packet of then-secret witness statements in December of 1963, believing him when he said his single motive was to act as devil's advocate for Oswald. "I want to represent this boy," Lane told me. "I don't think he did it." If I hadn't shared that packet with him, I wonder if people such as Lane, and later Jim Garrison and Oliver Stone, would be viewed today as brave souls who fought to bring the light of truth to the assassination story.

Lane, an attorney and one-term New York State Democratic assemblyman from the JFK wing of the party, published a lengthy piece in the *National Guardian* in early December laying out the alleged facts from which he'd concluded that Oswald could not have killed Kennedy. The story ran well before Lane ever visited Dallas, spoke to any witnesses or investigators, or contacted me. It was full of inaccuracies and unsupported suppositions.

When he first called me in December, I told him I was very busy but agreed to meet with him at my apartment the next evening.

"Do you know anybody who knows Jack Ruby well?" he asked.

I said that I knew Ruby well enough to intensely dislike him.

"Really?" Lane replied, his interest plainly apparent. "Well there's no doubt that he and Oswald were involved," he continued. "But we don't know exactly how." Then he mentioned he had an appointment scheduled for the next day with a Dallas business figure who had seen Oswald and Ruby plotting together, just a few weeks before the assassination. "I talked to him on the phone, and he sounds like the real thing," Lane told me.

"How many people have you interviewed so far?" I asked.

"Well you may be the first," he said. "Then this other source, this lawyer with an impeccable memory. Maybe I'll get to him tomorrow. But I will share it with you if you will help me."

"Who's footing the bill for your investigation?"

"I am, completely," he assured me. "I am certainly not in it for the money. This will cost me plenty, but I think it's very important."

Lane came by the apartment again the next morning. He said his good source, the one who could put Oswald and Ruby together in the Carousel Club, had bowed out for the time being. "He's had some threats," said Lane, "and he needs some time to think it over. We're going to talk again tomorrow."

At this point, I had not yet met Carroll Jarnagin. But I'd heard about him from Johnny King, who said the lawyer was "a nice-enough guy but a bad lush," and that he thought I should talk to Jarnagin eventually, if only to discount his story. "He's told us other stories." King laughed. "One about LBJ we would have loved to believe, another about John Tower. The guy gets around, especially in his own mind."

At this early stage in the story, I was still running down what at first often looked like great leads that connected Oswald with others in the shootings. It was too soon to dismiss possibilities. And under the general rule that even a blind pig can sometimes find an acorn, I was deeply curious to learn the identity of Lane's source, hardly prepared for whom he would turn out to be.

Lane tried to impress me with how much he knew about the assassination, which wasn't much at all. I'd recall this conversation three years later when I first sat down with Jim Garrison. The New Orleans DA didn't know much either. Lane would mention this source or that eye witness, and I would contradict him. "No, he didn't say that." Or, "She wasn't in a position to hear that."

"But how do you know?" he kept asking.

Because, I explained, in some cases I conducted the first interview with the individual in question or knew something about him or her that called their word into question. A lot of them changed their stories as time passed too.

"A few days after somebody got to them," Lane added in a conspiratorial voice.

There was another reason I was certain of my facts. "I know what they said to the cops too, within hours of the shootings," I said. "They might have refined the facts later, but I know what they originally said."

"What makes you so sure?" Lane asked.

Fool that I was, eager to prove my point to this opportunist, I went into the next room grabbed a stack of papers, came back, and tossed them on the coffee table. "There are the eyewitness accounts," I said, "made the afternoon of November 22."

Lane was amazed. "Where did you get these?"

I could not divulge my source, but the reports were authentic, I told him.

He began to read, and we didn't speak for a long time.

"The only reason I'm showing you these," I said at last, "is that you made many, many misinterpretations in your article. If you are truly interested in giving Oswald a fair shake from a historical standpoint, I think you need to know what the investigation shows so far."

"Oh, yes," Lane agreed.

He glanced at his watch and asked, "Could I use your telephone? I was supposed to call Oswald's mother about now. I'm meeting with her tomorrow and don't want to miss her or call too late."

"Are you representing her?" I asked, thinking back over my recent, testy confrontations with Marguerite.

"Not yet. But I intend to."

"Then be my guest," I said, and pointed out the telephone resting on a table in the next room.

Given the size of our apartment and the thickness of the walls, it was impossible not to overhear Lane's conversation even if I tried, which I didn't. Three or four times he said to her, "I really don't think it will make much difference."

"I couldn't help but hear, Mark," I said when he finished. "What was all that 'doesn't matter' stuff about?"

"Oh, she is quite an opinionated woman," he said. "She thinks Lee was a paid informant of the FBI, and she asked how much difference that would make. I told her it probably doesn't matter either way."

He changed the subject.

"You know, you are an important contributor to the truth in this case," Lane said, exuding sincerity. "Will you help me find the truth? I have to go back to New York in a day or so, and I was wondering if I could borrow these statements for a few days. I want to contact these people to see what, if any, pressure has been brought on them and if they have something different to say now."

All of these years later, I could still kick myself for what I said next:

"Of course, I'm not writing anything more about the witnesses, at least not for now."

I didn't even take the partial precaution of making Lane go photocopy the pages. In part, this was because copying was not so cheaply or simply done in 1963 as it is today. Public photocopy machines were not common. Plus, I had made good notes on all of the important witnesses.

Despite his promises, Lane did not immediately return the witness reports to me. But I was busy with other parts of the assassination story and saw no reason to distrust the earnest young lawyer from New York. I did call his office a few times. He was never in.

Then I began seeing wire service stories from Europe, reporting the fundraising activities of so-called "Who Killed Kennedy?" committees in Britain and across the continent. The dispatches said that the eminent British philosopher, Bertrand Russell, was involved with the committees and reported that Mark Lane was their executive director. I also read about Lane appearing at a press conference, waving a fistful of documents in the air and proclaiming that these papers proved that the witnesses in Dallas contradicted the authorities.

I had made a horrific mistake.

A few days later I received a telephone call from Bertrand Russell in London. "First," the old man said in a cultivated British accent, "I want to congratulate you for stealing all those statements from the Dallas police. I don't profess to understand how you did it, but you have done the world a great service."

Famous as he was, I confess to little detailed knowledge of Russell's contributions to the world of thought. I knew nothing of his politics, and I had no idea why he was calling me. I wasn't even positive, at first, whether it really was Bertrand Russell on the telephone or someone perpetrating a hoax. Stranger things have happened to me. Were it not for that aristocratic accent, I would have suspected I was hearing from some wag at the paper, but nobody I knew could have sustained such an accent for so long. I told Russell that I had not stolen anything from any investigative agency and I didn't know where anyone would get that idea, surely not from me.

"Oh, Mr. Lane informed me you would say just that," he replied with a chuckle.

Russell said he had some questions for me "about some of the stories you have written."

I advised him to submit his queries in writing and that I'd be pleased to answer them as best I could. This response did not make him happy. He seemed accustomed to people doing as he instructed. The conversation soon ended.

However over the ensuing months, he did write me three times, exploring all possibilities of official chicanery, falsification, and the like. The only subject I wouldn't touch was one I still refuse to touch today. I do not know how to explain Kennedy and Connally's wounds. The Warren Commission might be correct or perhaps totally wrong about its much-maligned single bullet theory, the belief that a single bullet slammed through the president's back and throat and then into Governor Connally. I do know that I heard three distinct shots that afternoon. So did several other people in Dealey Plaza whom I interviewed shortly thereafter.

On February 7, Lane finally responded to my repeated demands that he return the witness files. He also offered me a job as his investigator, assuring me in a letter that "our communications and contacts would be priviledged [sic] and I (Lane) need not divulge them to anybody."

I never answered his letter and thought I was through with him at that point. But less than a month later, Lane testified before the Warren Commission about his secret source: Carroll Jarnigan.

He told the commission that he considered his informant a "reliable and responsible" person who had participated in a meeting at the Carousel Club to plot the president's assassination. The alleged session was also attended by Ruby, Bernard Weismann, and J. D. Tippit! It took place a few days before the assassination, he said.

Lane told the commission that he would try to convince his informant to testify. Of course, that never happened. The commission pleaded with Lane and finally paid his airfare from Europe to testify. Still he would not divulge his source.

Perhaps Lane knew of Jarnagin's attempt to sell his ever-changing fantasy tale or had learned that Jarnagin utterly failed a polygraph exam administered by the district attorney's office. For whatever reason, Lane resisted naming him.

Chief Justice Warren didn't like that.

"We have been pursuing you," Warren said, "with letters and entreaties to give us that information so that we might verify what you have to say—if it is a fact or disproving if it is not a fact."

The surprise to me was not that Lane would not back up his tale. He had already made countless such assertions. I was more amazed at the commission's poor background investigation. Several people in Dallas were well aware of Jarnagin's mutable yarn and that he later admitted he'd fabricated everything.

Henry Wade and Chief Curry testified at length before the commission. No one thought to ask them about Jarnagin even though Wade had personally arranged for his lie detector test. The DA later told me, "it went off the charts—far off the charts."

This is the sort of evidence that Lane typically produced in support of his various conspiracy theories of the JFK case and, later, the assassination of the Reverend Martin Luther King Jr., which he argued was the work of off-duty FBI agents under J. Edgar Hoover's personal control.

To dismiss Lane's imaginative scenarios as rubbish, as I did at first, is to completely miss the point. Lane found that he could make almost any assertion about the assassination—even under oath—with impunity. He almost single-handedly invented the lucrative, still thriving, JFK conspiracy story business.

It's no wonder he and Marguerite got along so well.

His book, *Rush to Judgment*, was a mishmash of unproven and unlikely allegations and off-the-wall speculations. Fifteen publishing houses turned it down because they were too far behind Lane on the manufactured-controversy learning curve.

Only Holt, Rinehart and Winston guessed the true potential for profits in *Rush to Judgment*. They issued the book as a $5.95 hardback in 1966 and sold thirty thousand copies in just two weeks. It was a publishing home run, and it showed the way for hundreds of other buffs in their turn to advance their bogus claims, grab their fifteen minutes of notoriety, and also make a buck—sometimes lots of bucks—in the process.

For example, a West Texas man named Ricky White popped up one day with the story that his father, a Dallas cop, had been the shooter. Dave Perry, the assassination researcher and onetime conspiracy buff who, for three decades now, has used his comprehensive knowledge of the case to debunk posers who can't quite make their stories fit the facts, demonstrated that almost all of White's tale was pure fiction. Nonetheless Oliver Stone gave White $80,000 of his film *JFK*'s reported $40 million budget for his story.

In addition to Oswald, Ruby, and Lane, the fourth leg of the conspiracy chair was Jim Garrison, the unhinged New Orleans district attorney who, by virtue of his position, lent reassuring, official legitimacy to the wildest stories—reliable sanction for just about any crackpot claim.

As *Rush to Judgment* rocketed to the top of the bestseller lists in the autumn of 1966, Garrison happened to meet Louisiana Senator Russell Long on an airplane trip from Washington, D.C., to New Orleans. Long always believed there had been a conspiracy behind the 1935 assassination of his father, Huey Long, the famous governor of Louisiana nicknamed "The Kingfish." The senator harbored doubts about the Kennedy case too and urged Garrison to look into the matter. In late 1966, the district attorney began checking out volumes of the widely criticized Warren Commission report from his local library.

Fast forward to mid January 1967. Jack Ruby had just died of cancer. I was just starting my new job at *Newsweek*'s Houston bureau when I received a call from Garrison. He invited me over to discuss the Kennedy assassination. "I keep running into your name," he said. "I think you have information that could help me in an ongoing investigation, and I'm very sure I have information you would consider more than just interesting."

Jim Garrison—originally Earling Carothers Garrison—was first elected New Orleans DA in 1962. He built a reputation from the start as a crime and corruption fighter—he once indicted his predecessor—and was widely popular with both his constituents and the press. A few months before Big Jim, as he was known, first contacted me, writer Jim Phelan had published an admiring profile in *The Saturday Evening Post* of the hulking one-time FBI agent also sometimes called the Jolly Green Giant.

Garrison told me he thought I could "fill in some holes" for him. Sensing this might be the start of a great story, I agreed to what would become a long series of memorable encounters. The day I met Garrison was one of the strangest of my life.

He was then forty-five years old, about six feet six, chronically unkempt, and a little crazy around the eyes. He had a booming voice and swaggering manner, precisely the opposite of the sober character Kevin Costner portrayed in *JFK*. He dominated conversations with a sort of zigzag style of discourse that was both nutty and disturbing for the fact that a high-level, high-profile elected official could believe the nonsense that Garrison professed to believe.

He greeted me at his house in January 1967, a month after he secretly started his crusade. We began by looking over some photos of Dealey Plaza together. "Now, Hugh," Garrison would say in that rumbling mid-western baritone, "who are those people in this photo?"

I identified the ones that I recognized and shared what I knew of their roles and actions on the day of the assassination. Each time, Garrison growled, "You don't understand, Hugh. Let me tell you how this really came down!"

I argued with him a few times and then realized I was going to get thrown out on the street if I kept it up. If I wanted access to Garrison, I just needed to sit there and listen.

From time to time we were interrupted by the telephone. Garrison took the calls in an adjoining room, where I clearly heard him bellow strange phrases, such as "tiger fifteen," or "lion three," then abruptly hang up the receiver.

Finally, I had to ask. "Jim, I couldn't help but hear. What was that all about—the animals?"

"Ah, that's an old Navy code," he replied expansively, obviously very pleased with himself. "The Feebies will never break it."

At the time, I knew of no reason why the Feebies—the FBI— would be interested in Garrison's home telephone conversations or wouldn't know how to break an old Navy code if they were. On the evidence of that afternoon, I concluded the Big Easy's Green Giant was a troubled man, more likely of interest to psychiatrists than federal investigators.

"Hugh," he said at last, "you're lucky you're in town today. We've just verified this guy, and believe me it's dynamite." Explaining no more for the moment, Garrison then called one of his assistant DAs, ex-boxer Andrew Sciambra, known as Moo Moo, who arrived a short while later with Garrison's newly discovered star witness in tow. He was a slight little guy from Houston, a piano player, who proceeded to tell us how he knew that Ruby and Oswald were longtime gay lovers.

He went into great detail, naming clubs in Dallas and Houston where he said he had been performing when Ruby and Oswald dropped by. He even described one occasion when the owners of a Houston club had booted out the two of them "because," he said, "they had been groping each other all evening long."

Garrison beamed.

"You might be the most important witness we've run across yet," he told the piano player. "And you are certain they were with each other on several occasions?"

The little man vigorously nodded yes, clearly pleased that Garrison was buying his story.

"What do you think of that, Hugh?" the DA asked when his witness was finished. "Isn't this it?"

I mumbled something and stared closely at the man, certain that I'd seen him somewhere before. Then it came to me: I knew who he was! And I remembered where I had first seen him. He had come forward within three days of the assassination, telling exactly the same story to the Dallas police. When they didn't believe him and he failed a quickly arranged polygraph, the angry DPD detectives told him he was going to jail. The last I'd seen of the piano man, he was crying and scrambling out the police station door.

"What are you going to do with this guy, Jim?" I asked, even more bewildered than I had been at the goofy telephone code. "When are you going to announce this?"

"Due time," he answered. "We're putting our pieces together."

One of these pieces turned out to be Rodney Stalls, the wacky engineer and original conspiracy buff who showed up on my doorstep within hours of the assassination. UPI reporter H. G. "Doc"

Quigg told me that Stalls also approached him with what sounded like the same paper bundle of scribbled "proof" in the hallway of the criminal courts building in New Orleans.

"He said he had an appointment with Garrison later that day," Quigg recalled.

We both laughed.

Neither Stalls nor the Houston piano player lasted long in Garrison's good graces. As his theories morphed—and they did with each moon—his blockbuster witnesses changed as well. One of these was a former mental patient from the West Coast, a rangy character who wore a red toga and sandals and called himself Julius Caesar. Mr. Caesar claimed to have been present at a hotel in Alexandria, Louisiana, where Oswald met with Clay Shaw, the beleaguered New Orleans businessman whom Garrison would falsely prosecute for conspiracy to assassinate Kennedy. Caesar said he was there too when Jack Ruby arrived at the hotel with a package of cash for the other two.

For a brief time, Julius Caesar was the district attorney's special guest in New Orleans. When the inevitable rips and worn spots developed in his story, Garrison put his witness out on the street. In my one conversation with Julius Caesar, conducted on the courthouse steps, he made the even bolder claim to have participated in the assassination itself.

Then came Cedric Von Rollston, who said he met Oswald in a New York bowling alley and had come to adore "this cherubic, beautiful young man." Von Rollston assured Garrison that his personal relationship with Oswald was not sexual. However, he added, one of the Russian diplomats, a homosexual, was often with Oswald and lured the beautiful young man away.

Von Rollston traveled to New Orleans with an individual he described as his wife though she looked more like a brother or uncle. He kept Garrison's attention for a few days with tales of Russian intrigue, illicit sex, and secret assignments in which he claimed Oswald was involved. But eventually, Cedric, too, was banished from Garrison's A list.

Von Rollston telephoned me a few times, wanting to share with me the indignities he'd suffered at Garrison's hands. One day he said, "You know, if my father was alive, he wouldn't have the balls to treat me like this." Cedric, who was white, said his father was Paul Robeson, the famous black opera star.

Then there was Annie Patterson, an American behind bars in Mexico at the time. She told Garrison that if he helped free her, she would tell him all she knew about a scene she'd witnessed in a Laredo, Texas, bar room where Vice President Johnson met Oswald and handed him the cash to shoot Kennedy. When I later called her at the jail, she said that Clay Shaw was at the meeting too. I did a canvass of Laredo's bars but could not find one that remotely resembled the place Patterson described. Further checking showed that both Johnson and Shaw had attended public events far from Laredo on the day of the alleged meeting.

Thenceforth I refused Annie Patterson's collect calls.

The case that Jim Garrison finally took to court against Clay Shaw originated with a sometime journalist who called himself Jack Martin but in fact was a convicted felon who had changed his name from Edward Stewart Suggs.

Suggs belonged to a splinter religious group that boasted a total Louisiana membership of three: Suggs, a commercial pilot named David Ferrie, and one other individual. Ferrie was a bishop of this exclusive church. For no better reason than he coveted a title such as Ferrie's for himself, Suggs turned the pilot in as a suspect in the Kennedy assassination.

Ferrie, distinctive for being utterly hairless and for his bright red wig and matching eyebrows, might have made an interesting defendant had he not suddenly expired from a cerebral aneurysm on February 22, 1967. He had been fired a few years earlier by a major airline for sneaking a young boy into the cockpit with him on a flight. While there was little doubt as to his pedophilia, there was never any serious reason to believe David Ferrie was involved in the assassination.

His death shifted Garrison's focus to a rotund, oddball New Orleans attorney named Dean Andrews, who claimed that he had once represented Oswald in a couple of minor matters. Andrews further reported that he'd been contacted to represent Oswald again, just hours before Jack Ruby fired his fatal shot.

Andrews said that a man calling himself Clay Bertrand had telephoned to ask that he go to Dallas on the afternoon of Saturday, November 23, to act as Oswald's lawyer. The problem was that Andrews was in the New Orleans Hotel Dieu Hospital that afternoon, under heavy sedation in a room that lacked a telephone. In another version of the alleged telephone conversation, Andrews said the caller had been Marguerite Oswald. Andrews in time fully recanted his story. Garrison indicted him for perjury, and the jury convicted.

Nonetheless the DA decided to go after the phantom Bertrand. My friend, the late Bill Gurvich, once Garrison's chief investigator, told me his boss called a staff meeting in December 1966, where he announced he was determined to find "this homosexual Clay Bertrand fellow," whom Andrews had admitted was a fabrication. Clay Bertrand did not exist. What was more, Gurvich recalled his amazement when Garrison said he knew the man's real name was Clay, "because they never change their first name." The DA explained, "I learned that in intelligence."

The group consulted its collective knowledge of gay males living in the French Quarter, and someone mentioned Clay Shaw. On the strength of that alone, Shaw was questioned in late December 1966, not long before my first meeting with Garrison at his house.

Shaw denied ever meeting Oswald and any knowledge of the assassination. After Ferrie died two months later and Andrews refused to implicate Shaw in anything, the Green Giant was stymied. But only momentarily.

Just as Gurvich and the rest of Garrison's more professional assistants were urging him to drop the investigation altogether, a letter came from Perry Raymond Russo, a part-time insurance salesman and student in Baton Rouge who claimed to have known Ferrie—by then publicly identified as the DA's number one suspect—and wrote that he'd be glad to talk to Garrison.

Moo Moo Sciambra was dispatched to Baton Rouge at once to meet with Russo, who laid out a fantastic tale to the DA's man of meetings and parties where Ferrie had entertained Cuban freedom fighters as well as a man who looked a lot like Oswald.

Garrison was back in the game. He brought Russo to New Orleans, where several polygraph exams were administered. Russo failed them all. Undeterred, Garrison had Russo put under sodium pentathol, familiarly known as truth serum, and also ordered up a session with a hypnotist.

At first, it appeared that Garrison had finally hit pay dirt. Under hypnosis, Russo identified Clay Shaw as a participant in one of Ferrie's gatherings. However some months later, it came to light that the hypnotist had first described Shaw to Russo and urged him to weave the businessman into his account.

By this time, Bill Gurvich had repeatedly expressed his doubts to Garrison about the investigation and his own role in it. The DA had assigned Bill to tail people, dig in their trash cans, even photograph a Las Vegas nightclub act that Garrison thought might have a connection to Jack Ruby and his friends. There was no apparent method to Big Jim's madness.

"Can't you tell me what evidence we've got?" Gurvich would ask.

"We know who the assassins are," Garrison always replied, "and they can't get away. They know we will pursue them everywhere." Garrison never did specify who these shooters were although from time to time he indicated they were Cubans.

He continued to pursue every new lead, no matter how flimsy or preposterous. Nor was he above extralegal shenanigans. A local cat burglar even reported that the prosecution had approached him to plant evidence in Shaw's residence.

Yet despite Garrison's every effort to manufacture a more persuasive case against Shaw, Perry Russo by default became the DA's main witness and, unlike his ill-starred predecessors in that dubious role, remained so when Clay Shaw went to trial in early 1969. Russo, a manifestly flawed witness, was the best Garrison could do.

"It was so apparent that Perry was making it all up," Gurvich told me. "We tried to talk Jim out of continuing this stuff when Ferrie died. We told him, 'You will look good. Everybody knows Ferrie was your number one suspect. You can just say you solved it and walk away.'

"He wasn't buying that. He was already pumped up with the adoration of the conspiracy people and all. He was getting calls from all over the country, from Europe, even from Japan and Australia. He couldn't buy a meal in New Orleans or pay for a cab ride. He was exciting the whole town, and boy was he caught up in it."

Bill Gurvich was a talented and seasoned investigator, and Garrison apparently noted his disaffection with some concern. Alvin Oser, the assistant district attorney who later led the Shaw prosecution in court, told me that Bill argued "a bit too forcibly" in favor of shutting down the investigation after Ferrie's death.

Garrison, said Oser, "didn't think Bill was completely on board, but he didn't want to lose him."

So in an effort to keep Bill on the team—and thus avoid the embarrassment of a public resignation—Big Jim decided to share the spotlight with Gurvich, assigning him to make what Oser called "the big announcement"—the March 1, 1967, public disclosure that a surprise suspect, Clay Shaw, had been arrested for conspiring to kill President Kennedy.

Shaw was taken before the grand jury, where Garrison and his assistants put on dozens of witnesses, threatening several of them if their testimony strayed from the script. On March 22, after listening at length to Perry Russo weave his fairy tale, the jurors voted to indict Shaw for his alleged role in the assassination.

Gurvich saw that Garrison was coming unglued and by mid-1967 believed his boss capable of almost any outrage to keep the conspiracy juggernaut rolling. As Bill later told me, when Bobby Kennedy scheduled a trip to town, Garrison threatened, "If Bobby Kennedy set foot in his jurisdiction, he'd arrest his ass and see if that didn't force the government to come clean" with what it knew, and was withholding, about the assassination.

Gurvich secretly flew to New York at his own expense to meet with Kennedy, who was by then a U.S. senator with serious presidential prospects. He warned Kennedy not to risk such a Garrison stunt if he came to New Orleans.

Somebody tipped the Green Giant to Gurvich's mission. Before Bill could return, Garrison fired him, charged him with the "removal of a moveable"—the assassination investigative file, I guess—and locked him out of his office. There was no trial for the moveable removal, and Gurvich went on to provide invaluable assistance to Clay Shaw's legal defense.

———— ✠ ————

The seeds of my own inevitable rupture with Garrison were sown in March 1967 when I learned that Lynn Loisel and Louis Ivon, a pair of New Orleans cops assigned to Garrison, had offered a potential witness what sounded very much like a bribe. Within days of David Ferrie's death, Loisel and Ivon sought out newlywed Alvin Beauboeuf, a twenty-one-year-old gas station attendant who had been one of several young men who hung around with Ferrie. The two cops asked Beauboeuf to identify a snapshot of himself with Ferrie, which he did as he already had done three times before. Then, as Beauboeuf told the story, Loisel and Ivon said their boss, Jim Garrison, thought he, Beauboeuf, knew all about the assassination, which Beauboeuf denied.

According to Beauboeuf, his visitors then mentioned the DA's unlimited financial resources and how there might be a payment of up to $15,000 and even a job with an airline if he could help fill in some holes. Beauboeuf replied that he'd have to talk it over with his wife and promised to call Loisel the next day.

Instead he called his lawyer, Hugh Exnicios, who suggested they should get the offer on audiotape and then proceed accordingly. Exnicios telephoned Loisel and invited him over to his office in Jefferson Parish, west of downtown, where the lawyer would hide a tape recorder behind a curtain.

"Now let me bring you up to what Al and I were talking about last night," Loisel began. "I told him we had liberal expense money, and I said the boss is in a position to put him in a job, you know, possibly of his choosing, of Al's choosing. And there would be . . . We would make a hero out of him instead of a villain, you understand.

"Everything would be to your satisfaction. There's no . . . I mean we can . . . we can change the story around, you know, to positively beyond the shadow of a doubt, you know . . . eliminate him, you know, into any type of conspiracy or what have you."

Exnicios nodded and said nothing.

"The only thing we want is the truth, you know," Loisel went on. "No deviations on his part, you know. We want to present the truth. We want the facts and the facts of the assassination. That's what we want. And for this, the release you know. The thing will be typed up in such a way that Al, you know, will be free and clear."

Exnicios: "Now in other words, what you want him to do, he will come up and give you such evidence that you will be able to couch him in terms of being a hero?"

Loisel: "That's correct."

Exnicios: "And you'll also . . . you have an unlimited expense account, you said, and you're willing to help him along?"

Loisel: "I would venture to say, well I'm, you know, fairly certain we could put $3,000 on him just like that, you know. I'm sure we would help him financially, and I'm sure real quick we could get him a job."

They discussed the previous night's offer of a job with an airline.

"Al said he'd like a job with an airline, and I feel the job can be had," Loisel assured Exnicios. He mentioned an air freight company and said, "With just one phone call, he [Beauboeuf] could write his own ticket, you know."

The lawyer pointedly asked twice for the cop's guarantee that Garrison himself stood behind these offers. Loisel confirmed that he did.

Exnicios then asked how his client would be expected to help with the investigation.

"Well, first off," Loisel replied, "I feel . . . well, we feel that Al is as close to Dave [Ferrie] as anybody could have been. Alright, now we know this is rough . . . I'm drawing you a rough sketch. We have a man who has come forth recently, told us he was in a room with Ferrie, Shaw, two Cubans, and Oswald." Loisel said that this meeting was at Ferrie's house, and the topic was how to kill Kennedy in a crossfire. "I believe it was Clay Shaw and Ferrie," he said, "or maybe it was Clay Shaw and Oswald, having a little heated argument. Clay Shaw wanted some of his methods used, or thoughts, you know, used, but anyhow that's what we have in mind, along that line."

Loisel said he knew that Beauboeuf was not present at this meeting but added, "Well, Alan is in . . . Al being close to Ferrie, had to know the whole thing from the beginning to end. He has to know it."

Exnicios asked how Beauboeuf could avoid charges if he had concealed such knowledge for years.

"You understand now that poor Dave is gone," Loisel replied. "Al has voluntarily come forward and told of his knowledge. I mean, there's ninety-nine thousand ways we could skin that cat, you know. I mean, it's something you know . . . that's his patriotic duty."

Beauboeuf then repeated that he knew nothing of what Loisel was talking about, and the investigator departed. But that wasn't the end of the story.

It didn't take long for Garrison's office to learn that a tape existed of Loisel's conversation with Exnicios and Beauboeuf and that I was putting together a story for *Newsweek*. About eleven on the night of April 11, Loisel and his partner Ivon returned to Beauboeuf's residence, where the conversation soon turned mean.

"You know, Al, you play dirty politics you get hurt," said Loisel, according to Beauboeuf. He said the cop added, "Al, I don't want to get into any shit, and before I do, I'll put a hot load of lead up your ass."

Next day, Beauboeuf was summoned to the DA's office, where he signed a document saying that he did not consider the taped conversation an attempted bribe. The young man said he signed the paper after the investigators promised henceforth to leave him alone and also not distribute an embarrassing photo of him with Ferrie.

My *Newsweek* story, under the headline "The JFK 'Conspiracy,'" was published in the magazine's May 14, 1967, edition. I believe it was the first print piece to characterize Garrison broadly for what he was—a rabid wolf, both crazy and dangerous. I also described the factual case for conspiracy, which was then, as now, nonexistent. I detailed how Big Jim had used and discarded a parade of misfits, lowlifes, and others who were vulnerable because of skin color, ignorance, mental issues, accent, or sexual orientation. They were his obvious victims, but the circus in New Orleans also betrayed everyone who believed in the rule of law and trusted public servants to be honest and fair-minded.

Needless to say, my story disappointed the district attorney.

"Bare minimum," he told me face to face a few days after the article appeared, "you could find yourself before my grand jury. Perhaps more likely you could end up in a gutter somewhere."

On one level, the story prompted a classic official response in New Orleans. Garrison and everyone else implicated in his conspiracy to fabricate a conspiracy denied everything. A grand jury was convened to look into my disclosures. Nothing came of that. The New Orleans police department announced an investigation too.

A month later, the New Orleans *Times-Picayune* published the results of the official police review in a story by reporter Robert Ussery under the headline, "Pair Cleared in Bribe Probe" and subhead "Police Find No Violation in Beauboeuf Case." According to the article, Deputy Police Superintendent Presly J. Trosclair Jr., who said he had listened to the audiotape that Hugh Exnicios surreptitiously recorded of his conversation with Officer Lynn Loisel, declared that Loisel and Ivon "have not violated any rules of the code of conduct of the New Orleans police department."

Trosclair readily conceded at a press conference that the officers had admitted offering money and a job with an airline to Beauboeuf. The deputy superintendent said it was common practice for local, state, and federal officials to reward informants financially and added, "We do not interpret it as a violation."

Garrison threatened me in person and on the telephone. In one call, he said, "I hope *Newsweek* has good lawyers, and you may have a surprise when you come back to town," and then hung up. He also filed a complaint with the Louisiana state bar's ethics and grievance committee, charging that Alvin Beauboeuf's new lawyer, Burton Klein, was "leading a counterattack against an increasingly successful investigation by the district attorney's office."

The bar association ignored the charge.

Easily Garrison's most brazen lie in the Beauboeuf affair was his denial of the Exnicios tape, and he persisted in this fiction to his death. In his 1988 book, *On the Trail of the Assassins*, he wrote, "Aynesworth, who seemed a gentle and fair enough man when he interviewed me for several hours in my home, never did get around to revealing whose life our office had shortened. As for the $3,000 bribe, by the time I came across Aynesworth's revelation, the witness our office had supposedly offered it to, Alvin Babeouf [sic] had admitted to us that it never happened. Aynesworth, of course, never explained what he did with the 'evidence' alleged in his possession. And the so-called bribery tape recording had not, in fact, ever existed."

A few days before the scheduled start of Clay Shaw's conspiracy trial in January 1969, I obtained a copy of Garrison's witness list. There were approximately fifteen names on it, all but a couple of them familiar to me as the usual nut cases. I also knew this was no time for the defense to be complacent. The Green Giant may have had no factual case against Shaw, but he was masterful at pulling surprise witnesses out of his hat.

I suggested to F. Irvin Dymond, Shaw's lead counsel and one of Louisiana's best defense lawyers, that it would be wise to take a close look at unfamiliar names on the witness list. Among them was a Charles Spiesel, described only as a New York accountant. Dymond agreed it would be prudent to prepare for the unexpected, but when he raised the idea with Edward Wegmann, Shaw's longtime friend and civil lawyer who handled the defendant's finances, he was told that Shaw was nearly broke.

I persisted, introducing the defense team to a capable private investigator in Dallas who was willing to work for very little. In the end, Wegmann found the money, and they sent the PI off to New York to learn what he could about the CPA.

As I suspected, Charles Spiesel put on a bravura performance for the prosecution. Called to the stand just ahead of Perry Russo, under direct examination by Assistant Attorney James Alcock, Spiesel corroborated the story Russo was about to spin, testifying persuasively how he too had been present when Clay Shaw, Lee Harvey Oswald, David Ferrie, and others met in a French Quarter apartment to plot President Kennedy's murder.

Moe Waldron, covering the trial for the *Times*, at one point threw up his hands and left the courtroom. "No way this kook is telling the truth," said Waldron, "but that's the ballgame."

That was the consensus view among reporters.

James Kirkwood, the actor and writer covering the trial for *Playboy*, later wrote in *American Grotesque*, his book-length account of the case, "If James Alcock could have pressed a button and sent Spiesel careening out of the witness chair and back to New York at that very moment, no further questions asked, he would have been a most damaging witness."

There seemed no way to counter Spiesel's poised performance on the stand until just hours before the defense was to cross examine him. That's when the investigator from Dallas made his post-midnight return from New York with information that would ignite a bombshell under the accountant.

That morning in court, Dymond asked Spiesel about the $16 million lawsuit he'd filed. Spiesel replied in a matter-of-fact way that yes, he'd sued the New York City police, a detective agency, and a psychiatrist for hypnotizing him and ultimately ruining his business as well as his sex life.

"Why $16 million?" Dymond asked.

"One million for every year of the conspiracy," Spiesel explained.

"And are you the same Charles Spiesel who fingerprints his daughter when she comes to visit?"

"I certainly am."

"Why?"

"They always disguise themselves."

There was no "gotcha" moment in any of Spiesel's testimony, no verbal sparring with Dymond. Courtroom spectators were by now whispering and giggling, and the witness himself even smiled from time to time as he patiently recounted for the lawyer how he'd been hypnotized fifty or sixty times and that he knew detectives had followed him to New Orleans although he did not think they'd succeeded in hypnotizing him this time.

In the midst of this prosecution meltdown—two jurors later told me that, for them, it was the end of Garrison's case—James Kirkwood turned to me in the press seats and said, "At least he's not bleeding. He doesn't know that anything is wrong. He just keeps smiling."

Clay Shaw's jury was out for just an hour before returning a not-guilty verdict on March 1, 1969, two years to the day from his arrest. In *On the Trail of the Assassins*, Jim Garrison blamed Shaw's exoneration on the dark machinations of a devious defense. "I realized," he wrote, "that the clandestine operation of the opposition was so cynical, so sophisticated, and at the same time, so subtle, that destroying an old-fashioned state jury trial was very much like shooting fish in a barrel with a shotgun. The chief defense counsel uncannily seemed to know just what questions to ask Spiesel."

"For one very long moment," Garrison wrote, "while I am sure my face revealed no concern, I was swept by a feeling of nausea." If so, Big Jim perhaps employed some sort of ESP. He had left the courtroom before Dymond began questioning Spiesel.

As for why he put the accountant on the stand in the first place, Dymond told me he doubted whether Garrison thought to check out his witness's story. "He didn't want to know," said the defense lawyer. "Every witness he had was a flake, a liar, or an opportunist. No sense in confirming what they already suspected. They just didn't think we knew."

Though he was acquitted, Clay Shaw ended up broke. He later filed suit against Garrison for malicious prosecution but died of cancer before the case came to trial.

* * *

I detected surprisingly little public revulsion at Garrison's excesses or anger that a patently innocent man had been pilloried at enormous community cost. The complete collapse of the prosecution case should have promoted widespread skepticism at the conspiracy community's ceaseless intrigues, but it didn't. At best, the debacle in New Orleans only slowed their momentum.

Garrison himself weathered the humiliation well. At one point, a story went around New Orleans that the district attorney had molested a thirteen-year-old boy at a local health club. I interviewed the alleged victim's uncle and a police officer and found the charges believable. *Newsweek*, however, refused to use my reporting, so I gave it to the muckraking columnist Jack Anderson, who published the story on February 23, 1970. As far as I know, nothing further came of the case.

Garrison was charged in 1973 with taking bribes from the mob-related entertainment industry. He acted as his own attorney, arguing to the jury "the only reason I am on trial here is because I solved the Kennedy assassination." He was acquitted.

That year he also lost his bid for reelection against Harry Connick Sr., who went on to serve as Orleans Parish district attorney until he retired in 2002.

In 1978, Garrison was elected to the Louisiana State Circuit Court of Appeals. He was repeatedly reelected until his death from heart disease in 1992, the year after the premier of *JFK*, in which Oliver Stone cast him in a bit role as Chief Justice Warren.

The conspiracy buffs regrouped in 1975 when Mark Lane began lobbying members of congress to form what would become the House Select Committee on Assassinations. By his own estimate, Lane visited at least a hundred U.S. representatives, the first of whom were members of the House Black Caucus. Lane sold them on the select committee idea by suggesting a reinvestigation of not only the Kennedy assassination but also the murder of the Reverend Martin Luther King Jr.

The select committee was chaired by Congressman Louis Stokes of Ohio and led by lawyer G. Robert Blakey, chief counsel and staff director. The group toiled two years before concluding, on the basis of flawed and ultimately repudiated acoustic evidence, that Oswald may have fired three shots as is generally agreed but that a fourth shot was fired as well from the so-called grassy knoll. This one missed, according to the committee report's scenario.

With the acoustic results discredited and rejected by a panel of the National Academy of Sciences as well as other experts, there is no factual foundation to believe that a fourth shot was fired from anywhere in Dealey Plaza that day. The select committee also decided that a conspiracy obviously existed, though there was no indication in their report as to who had hatched such a plot, or why, or how.

G. Robert Blakey stepped up to fill in the holes—a popular phrase among the buffs. In his 1981 book, *The Plot to Kill the President*, written with Robert Billings, Blakey posits that Carlos Marcello, mafia don of New Orleans, ordered Kennedy hit in response to his administration's tough stand against organized crime.

Blakey's argument, shaky in a Jim Marrs sort of way, adduces evidence no more persuasive than the fact that Joseph Campisi, a well-known Dallas restaurateur acquainted with both Marcello and Jack Ruby, visited Ruby in jail just before his death in early 1967. Blakey suggests Campisi visited Ruby to convey Marcello's warning to keep his mouth shut.

Joe Tonahill of Ruby's defense team had a laugh at that notion. "Oh sure," said Tonahill. "The mob lets him live three years after he shot Oswald, allowed him to talk to hundreds of people. Then they threaten him?

"Be real."

Afterword

It is often said that in war the first casualty is truth. I can report
from firsthand experience that this also was the case for the
Kennedy assassination. The rifle shots had barely stopped
echoing over Dealey Plaza that Friday afternoon a half century
ago before untruths, both innocent and deliberate, began to
distort the record and creep uncorrected into the world's collective
consciousness.

Factual mistakes, of course, were inevitable. We in the press were
overwhelmed at first by a flood of disparate and often contradictory
information upon which our organizations performed a sort of
triage before passing the news along as quickly as possible to a world
eager for any word of the tragedy. Also from the very start, there
were individuals and groups—some secretive, others not—with
agendas and interests in framing the narrative from their perspective.
Finally, there were the delusional souls and cynical opportunists
who instantly swarmed with their invented anecdotes and theories,
drawn like moths to the white heat of a national disaster.

Newsgathering and analysis in a free society is an ongoing process that ideally should act in the manner of a wiki to self-correct over time. According to this view, the more people available to review and assess the known facts repeatedly—and challenge the alleged ones—the more likely their collective effort will lead to a credible narrative intelligent and thoughtful people can weigh and accept or reject.

Most important, this is an open process. If you claim to have hidden knowledge with revolutionary implications, you must present it for examination and debate. It is similar to how science weeds out errors and lies. It is the reason we no longer think the sun revolves around the Earth and have stopped burning witches.

That is not to say that a single, official interpretation of the facts is necessary or even desirable. We Americans still debate the meaning of the Constitution, the Civil War, the Great Depression, and all the other milestones in our history. From this constant reexamination of what is known, we continue to gain insight.

Like many national crises before and after, the Kennedy assassination seemed to start simply enough: Several rifle shots rang out, and the president was dead. But like other such monstrous calamities, it soon moved both forward and backward in time, sweeping together a global cast of characters as it mushroomed into a mammoth and complex saga. Subplots proliferated. Careers were made and ruined. The course of history and our perception of it have been permanently changed by what occurred.

Yet unlike our experience with other, similarly vast upheavals, we still do not agree on what actually happened. Paradoxically, it seems, a majority of Americans reject the only assassination narrative that is supported by the known facts of the case.

They are these: Lee Harvey Oswald acted alone, and Jack Ruby was in no way connected with him. Moreover, and possibly contrary to what you have heard or read or believe, there is nothing anywhere—no assertion, no alleged proof—that conclusively indicates otherwise.

I wish this were not so. I sometimes feel like the traffic cop at the scene of a wreck, standing out in the rain, waving my flashlight and advising the rubberneckers to "move along folks. Nothing to see here."

I certainly have heard some fascinating and inventive tales, and were they not inconveniently untrue, they would have been much more exciting for me to report and write about than the "sorry, no cigar" pieces that routinely have enraged my detractors over the decades.

Finally I have never disputed the possibility of a conspiracy, or conspiracies, behind the Kennedy assassination. Do not doubt that's a story I'd love to break. However the proof of such a plot continues to elude us. Like it or not, that leaves us with the record as it stands.

So let me add, after fifty years of covering the Kennedy assassination, I am open to any new information if it comes to light and would welcome it no matter where it would lead.

PHOTOS

Hardly a hearty welcome: the *Dallas Morning News* ad
and fliers strewn all over Dallas before Mr. Kennedy's visit.

213

JFK begins the day at a Fort Worth breakfast.

Smiles are all around as the day begins happily.

SECRET SERVICE HAS STEAK
IN PROTECTION OF KENNEDY

President Kennedy will get a thick, juicy steak when he
visits Dallas Friday. But some of the 2,000 guests at his Dallas
Trade Mart luncheon may get thicker, juicier steaks.

It won't be the result of any Republican plot.

The Secret Service wants it that way.

A spokesman for the sponsoring organizations said Wednes-
day Secret Service agents vetoed a proposal that cooks select
the choicest cut and broil it to the President's liking.

"They said they wanted the waiter to pick out a steak at
random after they've all been broiled and carry it to the
President," the spokesman related. "This was done, obviously,
for security reasons. A would-be assassin couldn't be sure of
poisoning the President's meal unless he put poison in every
steak served at the luncheon."

THE MENU
Fresh Fruit Cup
Top Sirloin Club Steak (8 ounces)
Tossed Green Salad
French-Cut Green Beans Almondine
Rolls and Butter
Apple Pie
Coffee

Tom Dillard/Dallas Morning News

Tom Dillard/Dallas Morning News

Warm arrival at Dallas Love Field.

Relaxed moments as the motorcade
begins at Love Field.

Exuberant crowds, many deep, along Main Street.

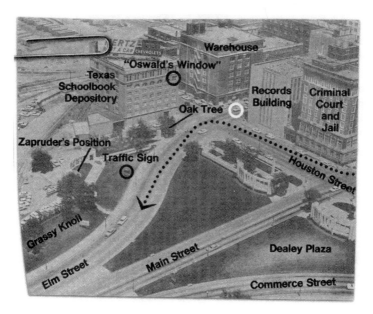

The parade route.

Dallas detective L. D. Montgomery carries the sack in which authorities claim Oswald carried his rifle to work that day. Detective Marvin Johnson is at right.

217

Helen Markham, up close, watched
Oswald shoot Police Officer J. D. Tippit.

A crowd gathers at the Tippit murder scene.

Larry Grove/Dallas Morning News

Cab driver William Scoggins tells the
author that Oswald tipped him a nickel.

Bob Jackson/Dallas Times Herald

Cabbie Scoggins and bus driver Cecil
J. McWatters wait to be interviewed
by homicide detectives.

Dallas Morning News exclusive, detailing Oswald's escape route, published five days after the assassination.

Larry Grove/*Dallas Morning News*

The author at the Texas Theater and the Tippit murder scene.

Dallas Police Chief Jesse Curry
at an early press briefing.

A defiant Oswald is brought through
newsmen for further interviews.

Lady Bird and LBJ console Jackie Kennedy.

Homicide chief Captain Will Fritz,
interviewed by Bill Mercer of KRLD Radio.

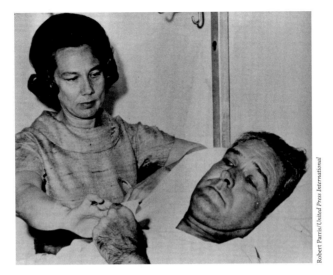

Governor Connally, after surgery at Parkland
Hospital, comforted by his wife, Nellie.

Marina Oswald escorted by a
Dallas detective to visit Lee.

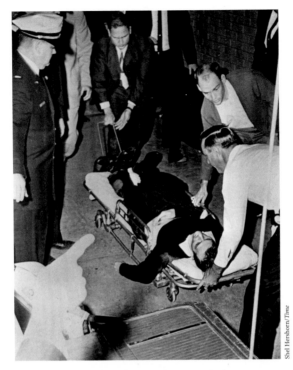

A dying Oswald loaded into ambulance
near the spot where he had been shot.

Marguerite and Marina Oswald at the police station.
Dallas Morning News reporter Kent Biffle behind them.

Jack Beers's story of his brilliant shot of Jack Ruby approaching Oswald, taken less than a second before the bullet hit the shackled prisoner.

Dallas Times Herald photographer Bob Jackson (shown here reloading his camera) shot a photo after Beers and won the Pulitzer Prize for his depiction of Oswald grimacing.

A typical noon press briefing during the Ruby trial.
The author at far left. Dorothy Kilgallen is to the
left of Ruby's lawyer Melvin Belli.

Montage of Marina, her child, and the author and
the story of her plea for clemency for Ruby.

Tom Dillard/*Dallas Morning News*

The *Dallas Morning News* covers Ruby's conviction.

Marina tells of her love for Lee.

Marina with Rachel and June Lee.

Jean Stafford had some interesting
moments with Oswald's mother.

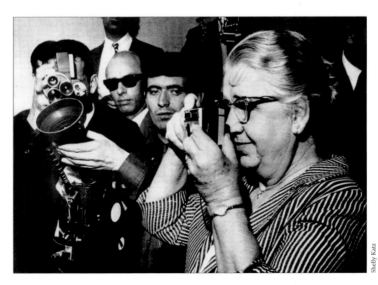

Marguerite Oswald at the Ruby trial, already
proclaiming her son's innocence.

Reports that fueled a bitter feud between
Dallas police and the FBI for years.

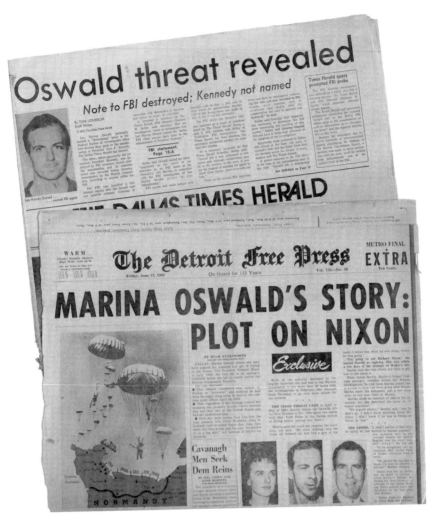

Oswald considered shooting Richard Nixon; the FBI destroyed
a note he left, causing further confusion and distrust.

Cover of the author's exclusive story in
Life magazine, June 1964.

Two *Dallas Morning News* exclusives

Letter to the author from Mark Lane, one of the early
conspiracy theorists who ignored many facts to gain
considerable attention—and money.

The New Orleans district attorney manufactured a case against
Clay Shaw, who was found innocent in less than an hour.

The *Dallas Morning News* decided against a special edition and published in-depth reportage Saturday morning, November 23, 1963.

The front page of the *Washington Times* twenty-five years afterward. At the bottom, the *Dallas Times Herald* edition printed within three hours of the tragedy.

Bob Oswald, Jim Leavelle, and ex-ABC newsman Murphy Martin (left to right) after lunch in Wichita Falls, Texas, a few years ago.

Sometimes a reporter just has to stop and ponder what's happened.

236

Index

Carswell Air Force Base, 13, 166
Carter, Cliff, 77
Carter, George, 44–45
Castleberry, Vivian, 42
CBS, 82, 162–164, 169, 171–172
Citizens Council, 70
Clark, Kemp, 18, 28
Clark, Kyle, 46
Clements, Manny, 131–132
Cobo Hall, 148
Coca-Cola, 23
Cochran, Mike, 12, 101–102, 136–137,
    166–167, 169
Cocke, Ed, 6
Cohen, Jerry, 170
Communist Party, 89
Conde, Carlos, 75
Connally, John, 3, 5, 9, 11, 14–15, 18, 68,
    70, 87, 167, 188, 223
Connally, Nellie, 9, 14–15, 223
Connick, Harry, Sr., 207
Conservatism USA, 9
Considine, Bob, 150, 173, 175–176
Cooper, John Sherman, 127
Costner, Kevin, 192
Covert, Sharon, 172
Crafard, Larry, 87, 89
Cronkite, Walter, 169
Croy, Kenneth, 28
Crull, Elgin, 97
Crume, Paul, 66, 145
Cry of Battle, 34
Cuban Missile Crisis, 2
Curry, Jesse, 12–13, 18, 40, 43–44, 70,
    81–83, 97–99, 116, 178, 189, 221

D
Dallas City Council, 71
Dallas Cowboys, 7
Dallas Greyhound Bus Terminal, 62
Dallas Ministerial Alliance, 76
Dallas Morning News, 1, 213, 220, 224, 227,
    232, 234, 243
Dallas Police Department, 29, 78, 94, 153,
    164
Dallas Press Club, 55
Dallas Times Herald, 9, 225, 235
Dallas Trade Mart, 1–2, 76, 165
Dallas Transit Company, 59
Davis, Barbara Jeanette, 26
Davis, Virginia, 26
Dealey Plaza, 12–13, 15, 19, 22, 24, 31–32,
    39, 43, 76, 82, 90, 123, 141, 165, 189,
    192, 208–209
Dealey, Ted, 5, 69, 131, 133
Dean, Patrick, 153
The Death of the President, 124

Decker, J. E. "Bill," 12, 82, 156
Detroit Free Press, 109, 134
Dootch Motors, 24, 26–27
Dowe, Ken, 90
Dudley M. Hughes Funeral Home, 27
Dudman, Richard, 169
Dudney, Bob, 45, 48, 171–172
Dugard, Martin, 176
Dulles, Allen, 128, 131
Dymond, F. Irvin, 204– 206

E
Eatwell Restaurant, 23
Eddowes, Michael, 161
Ekdahl, Edwin A., 103
Ellis, Luke, 141
Empire State Bank, 16
Esquire, 113
Ewell, Jim, 21–22, 39, 49, 108
Executive Inn, 115
Exnicios, Hugh, 200– 203

F
Federal Bureau of Investigation (FBI),
    17, 31, 37–48, 69, 77–78, 81, 94, 104,
    106, 108–110, 115, 119–120, 131–133,
    153, 169, 171–172, 179, 187, 190–192,
    230–231
Fenley, Bob, 54–55, 117, 153
Fenner, Nannie Lee, 46
Ferrie, David, 195–199, 201–202, 204
Flemmons, Jerry, 102
Flow Hospital, 61
Ford, Gerald, 81
Foreman, Percy, 146–148
Fort Worth Council of Churches, 101
Foster, Bill, 164
Fowler, Clayton "Red," 154
Fort Worth Press, 37
Fort Worth Press Club, 166
Frazier, Buell, 58, 80
Freund, Carl, 2, 145
Fritz, Will, 44, 77–78, 83, 98, 222
Frontline, 104
Fulbright, J. William, 5–6
Fuller, George A., 157

G
Gallup Poll, 3
Gander, Rod, 157, 160
Garage, Nichols, 89–90, 92
Garfield, James A., 81
Garner, Darrell Wayne "Dago," 174–176
Garrison, Earling Carothers "Jim," 114,
    170–171, 176, 184–185, 191–192, 195,
    199, 201– 203, 206–207
Gemberling, Bob, 40

About the Author

F our-time Pulitzer Prize finalist, bureau chief of both *Newsweek* and the *Washington Times*, and investigative team leader for ABC's *20/20*, Hugh Aynesworth was a thirty-two-year-old reporter for the *Dallas Morning News* when JFK's visit to Dallas ended in tragedy. His coverage of the assassination, the trial of Jack Ruby, and the conspiracy flurry that followed earned him two Pulitzer nominations and recognition as one of the most respected authorities on the Kennedy assassination.

His reporting of Martin Luther King's assassination, the 1993 Branch Davidian standoff and fire, and the 1995 bombing of the federal building in Oklahoma City marked his career advancement from a small-town sports editor to bureau chief. Aynesworth is the author or coauthor of seven books, including *The Only Living Witness* and *Conversations with a Killer* about serial murderer Ted Bundy. He has served as president of the Dallas Press Club and the Press Club Foundation and has won over seventy local, regional, and national awards.

Hugh Aynesworth lives in Dallas with his wife Paula, a sales executive at KERA and KXT North Texas Public Media.